THE LITTLE BOOK OF
SHARKS

This edition first published in the UK in 2008
By Green Umbrella Publishing

© Green Umbrella Publishing 2008

Publishers Jules Gammond and Vanessa Gardner

Printed and bound in China

ISBN 978-1-905828-27-2

Contents

Chapter 1

Introduction

OF ALL THE CREATURES IN THE animal kingdom, sharks are one of the few that have survived since long before the dinosaurs roamed the earth. As sharks are made of cartilage they do not fossilise well, but scientists and experts have been able to establish that this incredible fish was prevalent in the earth's oceans more than 350 million years ago from fossilised teeth and rare skin impressions.

They first appeared in the Silurian period – the age of fishes – and what we do know about them is that their bodies are streamlined to enable them to swim without using a great deal of energy. This is probably because sharks don't really sleep although they do have times of inactivity – nurse sharks have been observed resting motionless on the sea bed – they never stop swimming. They are kept buoyant by a huge liver, rather than a swim bladder like other fish and, if a shark stops swimming it will sink or stop breathing.

Sharks – as cartilaginous fish – are classed as Chondrichthyes which is split into two sub-classes. Sharks, skates and rays belong to the sub-class Elasmobranches, while ratfish and chimaeras belong to the sub-class

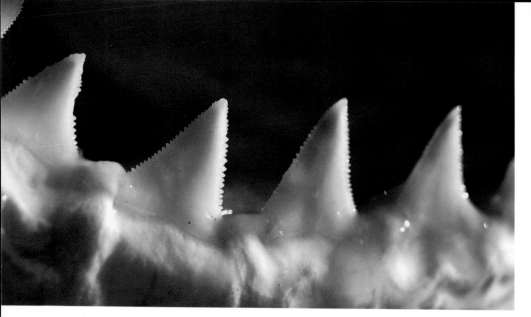

Holocephali. In the animal kingdom, sharks are from the sub-kingdom, metazoans, meaning many celled. The earth's oldest and largest habitat is its marine environment, where salt waters cover more than two-thirds of the world's surface. Not surprising then that it took man more than four million years to discover the megamouth. This shark had managed to remain undetected until 1976 when a US Navy ship hooked this huge shark nearly 15 feet long and weighing 1,650 lbs off the coast of Hawaii.

Although mainly confined to oceans, some sharks can be found in lakes and rivers. Bony fish including barracuda, tuna and virtually any other type of fish are able to swim forwards and backwards. A shark can only swim forwards. However, sharks vary greatly in their size, shape and habitats. There are about 368 species of shark and most are predators. The spined pygmy shark measures about seven inches while the whale shark can reach up to 50 feet long. However, most are medium-sized and measure between five and seven feet. All are grouped within 30 families and while some are rare, such as the great white, others like the bull shark are fairly common. While most sharks are torpedo-shaped, some species are quite unusual to look at. The angel shark has a flattened body so it can hide easily under sand, while the cookie cutter shark has an elongated body. Others, like the saw sharks have long snouts and some have large upper tail fins for stunning prey, such as the thresher shark. The hammerhead species have peculiar looking, wide heads.

Hunting takes place after dusk for most sharks and the majority of species feed on other fish. However, the larger species will also feed on larger marine animals including seals, dolphins, turtles and sea lions. Bull sharks are renowned for eating other sharks while hammerhead sharks are partial to stingrays and dogfish sharks eat lobster and crab. Tiger sharks are more opportunistic feeders than other sharks and will also eat carrion. There are two main methods that sharks use to feed. One is bottom feeding where the upper teeth are used to catch and hold onto prey. The other is filter feeding where huge quantities of plankton are filtered by gill rakers. The megamouth shark and bask-

ing shark use this method, swimming along with their mouths open in order to catch plankton and tiny fish. Teeth are not used to chew food, and sharks gulp food down in huge pieces that are then digested very slowly. Occasionally, a group of sharks will go on a feeding frenzy and will attack a food source – including a school of fish – together. This is a wild event and often the sharks end up attacking and eating each other.

After mating, fertilisation takes place inside the female who may then lay eggs (oviparous), bear live young (viviparous) or have eggs which hatch inside the mother (ovoviviparous). These fas-

cinating sea creatures mature at about the same rate as a human, although some mature into adults during their teenage years. They have a never-ending supply of teeth and if they lose some they are replaced quickly. Some sharks may have up to 3,000 teeth at one time set in up to five rows. The six senses, which these fish possess are vision, sight, smell, taste, vibration and electro-perception. Sharks are sensitive to the electric field that travels through the world's seas and oceans from active animal muscles. This electric sense helps the shark to navigate at night or in cloudy water. It also helps locate prey.

The habitats of sharks vary depending on the type of shark involved. Some live near the surface of the world's oceans and seas while others live in much deeper waters. Sharks living at the surface – or open water – are referred to as pelagic (including great whites, bull sharks and basking sharks), while benthic sharks like zebra horn sharks and wobbegongs live on the ocean floor. Despite being a sea fish, bull sharks have been known to travel up river into fresh water in the Amazon and also into the Mississippi River in the US. Some are strictly warm water fish including ham-

merheads and tiger sharks while others such as basking sharks and thresher sharks can be found in temperate waters. Dogfish sharks and goblin sharks are known to live in much cooler waters and while some sharks will live in one place their entire lives, others are renowned for travelling across oceans. Sharks that do not migrate are known as "local sharks" and have a habitat range of roughly 100 miles. Coastal pelagic sharks are capable of migrating more than 1,000 miles while the blue shark and the mako shark, known as "highly pelagic sharks" are renowned for migrating across oceans.

There is no definitive way to tell the age of a shark. As they lose their teeth regularly this method is unusable and sharks grow slowly compared with other marine life and animals. The variations between growth rates, even between populations of the same species, are so considerable that even using growth rings that occur on the vertebrae of some sharks is not a guarantee. Some sharks even stop developing growth rings in later life. Tagging sharks is now a popular way to monitor shark populations and growth rates in some areas of the world.

Many species of shark are extinct. Fossils of teeth – which contain bone and so fossilises – have shown that primitive sharks, known as cladodonts existed 100 million years before dinosaurs. These early fish had double-pointed teeth and grew to around three feet long. Extinct sharks include cladoselache sharks, stethacanthus sharks, orthacanthus sharks and hybodus sharks. The megalodon shark was the largest of the primitive sharks and could measure up to 40 feet – however this is an estimate based on looking at fossilised teeth. It was a meat-eating predator with teeth roughly three times the size of that of a great white. It swam in the world's ocean around 1.6 million years ago. Modern sharks have evolved from these early species and share a common ancestry with rays.

Rays are closely related to sharks although they look more like the flattened angel shark than the great white. They are a flat fish that evolved from sharks and are either seen in large groups or are solitary depending on the species. Like sharks, rays have cartilage rather than bone and many species have poisonous spines, such as the stingray, which is used to stun its prey. Also, like sharks, the size of rays varies enormously from the short nose electric ray which is roughly four inches wide and weighs one pound to the largest of the ray, the manta, which is in excess of 22

feet across and may weigh up to thousands of pounds. There are roughly 500 different species of rays.

Most sharks more than six feet long are a potential danger, but three in particular have a reputation for their viciousness, these are the great white, bull and tiger shark. The bull shark has carried out more attacks than most mainly because it likes to swim in more shallow water – where swimmers are then at risk – but the oceanic whitetip shark is also a dangerous hazard. Other sharks known to have attacked people include the blue shark, hammerhead shark, mako shark, grey shark, blacktip reef shark, lemon shark, spitting shark and the sand tiger. But, man kills more sharks each year than sharks kill man and most sharks would rather avoid contact with humans if at all possible. Even as predators, sharks are only likely to attack if they feel threatened or provoked in some way and occasionally attack due to mistaken identity. But attacks are rare and it is even rarer for the attack to be fatal.

Critically endangered species of shark include the grey nurse shark and the speartooth shark, while the northern river shark is listed as being short in numbers. Many other species of sharks are vulnerable if not endangered, including whale sharks and great whites. Other sharks that are listed endangered include the borneo shark, whitefin topeshark, angular angel shark, smoothback angel shark, spinner shark, pondicherry shark, smoothtooth blacktip shark, dusky shark, gulper shark, school shark or tope shark, bluegrey carpet shark, porbeagle shark and the ganges shark.

Despite the sharks' incredible evolutionary stability, they have been under threat for a number of different reasons including loss of habitat, drift nets and depleted food sources – due to overfishing – as well as being hunted for their bodies, meat and fins. Education has led to increased awareness of the plight of the shark and man is now trying to turn the tables to stop their demise. Governments are slow to issue fishing quotas to ease the problem of over-fishing, however, there is legislation to limit or ban trade in sharks and the IUCN (International Union for Conservation of Nature and Natural Resources) and the World Conservation Union are working hard to stabilise shark populations worldwide.

Chapter 2

Angel Shark

LIKE THEIR CLOSE RELATIVES, THE rays and the skates, angel sharks are flat-bodied from top to bottom with their eyes and spiracles (for respiration) located on top of their heads. These sharks may even be the evolutionary link between sharks and rays. They have a blunt snout and are cleverly camouflaged to enable them to lie, undetected, just below the surface of the sand with only their eyes and the very top of their body exposed. The long, wide fins to either side of its body gives the angel shark its name although it is also known as the monk shark, sand devil – for the nasty bite it may give – and monkfish. The sharks are tan with brown markings.

These unusual sharks have five pairs of gill slits which are located on the ventral surface and two dorsal fins. The mouth is found at the tip of the snout which is made of fleshy nasal barbells. It does not possess an anal fin. While the front end of the body is broad and flat, the rear part of the body has a muscular appearance which is more in line with other sharks. Its pectoral and pelvic fins are large and held horizontally.

The shark's teeth are small and extremely sharp, encased in trap-like jaws. Angel sharks vary in size from small, to the Pacific angel shark which is roughly five feet long, to the larger species which grow to around six and a half feet long. The shark is mostly found between 10 feet and 4,300 feet deep within the eastern Pacific Ocean – from Alaska to California in the US and from Ecuador to southern Chile in South America. They prefer warm temperate oceans and thrive in the southern hemisphere. Some angel sharks are migratory and off the eastern US coast, the

Atlantic angel shark enters more shallow waters during spring and summer.

As a benthic fish – meaning it lives on the bottom of the ocean – this shark spends its day hidden in the sand and rocks of the ocean bed waiting for passing fish, crustaceans and molluscs which it ambushes (angel sharks are extremely fast swimmers) and catches within its jaws. Angel sharks, like many other species of shark, are hunters by night, swimming along the reefs in search of prey. Although they hunt after dusk, their activity increases significantly after midnight. They have often been compared to the slow-moving,

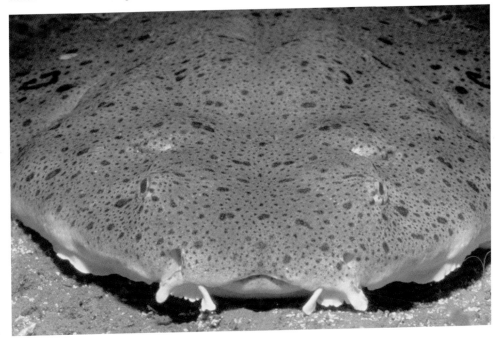

closely related skate, however even after lying for a number of weeks under the sand and mud of the ocean bed, these sharks are notoriously fast when a favoured prey comes within striking distance.

Little is known about the mating habits of sharks, although it has been observed that mating may take up to half an hour. It is not clear whether angel shark females only mate with one male, or whether males mate with more than one female. After mating, the female carries the eggs inside her body before the young are hatched and born live. As an ovoviviparous, the female angel shark retains the eggs inside her body until they hatch. Eggs are kept in the oviducts and have a thin membrane-like covering which does not thicken into proper egg cases. Embryos live on food supplies contained in the eggs in a temperature-controlled environment with little danger from predators. Once the food supply is finished the eggs hatch.

Litters will stay together until the pups are big enough to fend for themselves. This helps the young survive from predators including other sharks. Litters typically consist of eight to 13 pups. Females in all shark species show no interest in their young and pups are left to fend for themselves. Having been hatched inside their mother, angel shark pups are likely to be larger than other shark species that were laid as eggs and hatched outside their mother's body. Angel sharks grow slowly and feed on prey which is suited to their size – they need to be able to overpower prey in order to catch and eat it. These young are generally confined to the cover of the sea bed where they can easily stay camouflaged and out of danger giving them a much higher chance of survival.

Despite the fact that several species of angel shark are endangered or listed as vulnerable, the fish is frequently caught for food – one fish processor in California severely damaged the population in the region. Today, the fishing industry is regulated. They were declared a critically endangered species by the World Conservation Union due to their rapidly declining numbers. In some areas, including the North Sea, their demise has been so great that they are now extinct. Not known for being aggressive, if stepped on or captured, the angel shark is renowned for giving a nasty bite.

Chapter 3

Basking Shark

THE FIRST BASKING SHARK WAS spotted off the coast of Norway in 1765. After the whale shark, the basking shark is thought to be the second largest fish in the sea sometimes reaching lengths of up to 10 metres. This giant fish is a filter feeder and relies heavily on copious amounts of plankton and small marine animals to fulfil its dietary requirements. In order to feed successfully, the basking shark has five enormous gill slits that seem to virtually encircle its head while thousands of bristle-like "gill rakers" cover the gill arches within the slits. With its large pointed snout and huge dorsal and pectoral fins (often reaching up to two metres in length) the basking shark has a particularly distinctive shape.

The shark's body is a greyish brown and often has a paler colour underneath. The body is covered with mucus and its huge tail is shaped like a crescent moon. Its large mouth – which may measure up to one metre across – is filled with small hooked teeth which like all other sharks' teeth, are replaced regularly. However, despite its ferocious pre-historic appearance, the basking shark is actually a gentle giant.

While sharks do not have swim bladders, they are kept buoyant by their livers. The basking shark's liver, which is rich in light-weight oils, is particularly large and can weigh up to 25% of the total body weight. The liver contains a fatty substance known as squalene which, like most oils, is lighter than water. This is the basking shark's best buoyancy aid, running the entire length of its abdomen. Its cartilage (and not bone) structure is another buoyant aid.

The shark takes its name from its slow feeding pattern where it is often described as "basking" on the surface of

the water. Other names for this enormous shark include bone shark, elephant shark and sun fish. The basking shark takes up to 2,000 tons of water per hour to successfully feed and it does not seem to actively seek its food, but rather to rely on the water that is pushed through the gills. Feeding speeds are around two knots.

The largest known basking shark which was caught accidentally off the Bay of Fundy in Canada in 1851, measured more than 40 feet while it weighed more than 16 tons. The average length of this shark is between 20 feet and 28 feet and anything over this length is rare due to over-fishing.

Basking sharks are native the world over and prefer the cool and temperate waters of the earth's oceans with temperatures between 8ºC and 14ºC. The basking shark will often swim close to shore and is not afraid to enter an enclosed bay. Some of these sharks

have been found in tropical waters, but not in abundance. These sharks are open water sharks and are found at the surface of coastal waters during the summer months where they feed on copepods, but they do migrate offshore and deeper down in the ocean during winter months.

They are mainly solitary creatures, although they have been spotted in pairs and even large groups which are segregated by sex. Little is really known about their behaviour and when basking sharks "disappear" during the winter months, some experts have suggested that they might indulge in a form of hibernation. Scientific tracking however refutes this idea and indicates that basking sharks the world over migrate throughout the year. The only pregnant female to have ever been observed gave birth to six live young and it is believed that these sharks are ovoviviparous – developing eggs which hatch inside the mother – and only give birth every two to four years.

This enormous giant does not have many enemies however it is often attacked by lampreys, eel-like fishes that have a jawless mouth filled with rows of thorn-like teeth. In bony fish, lampreys are able to rasp into the fish's skin and with their sucker-like mouths feed from the fish's flesh. However, it is doubtful that this parasite is able to break through the shark's tough skin. A particularly vicious enemy of this shark is the tiger shark which is known to kill and eat basking sharks.

The basking shark does not mature quickly and given its slow reproductive rate has now been accepted on to the Convention on International Trade in Endangered Species' list for reducing trade of this fish and its body parts. Traditionally, the Japanese have used the shark's liver as an aphrodisiac, while in the west, the oils from this massive vital organ were used in cosmetics and lighting. The shark was, and still is, particularly vulnerable to over-fishing and repeatedly targeted populations are extremely slow to recover from their decline in numbers. Conservationists are urgently trying to gather data and information on this great shark in order to monitor it effectively and make strategic plans to protect it. Basking sharks are not particularly interested in humans and are harmless if left alone. They will usually evade a passing boat if at all possible.

Chapter 4

Bigeye Sixgill Shark

THERE IS CONFUSION AS TO WHEN the bigeye sixgill shark was actually discovered and documented. It was originally claimed to be in 1962 but recent events have put this seven years later when it was given the name Hexanchus nakamurai. Hexanchus comes from the Greek era meaning six and agcho meaning narrow but it is also known as the lesser sixgill and the calf shark.

The Hexanchiformes order is the oldest and most distinguishable of all sharks in that the members have six or seven gill slits rather than the modern shark's five. The bigeye sixgill shark does not portray the image of a typical modern shark as it possesses a hump where the main dorsal fin should be and only has one small dorsal fin between this hump and the tail. The caudal fin (tail) has an elongated upper lobe that stretches backwards while the anal fin is smaller than the dorsal fin. Considered a throwback to prehistoric times, the shark has six gill slits instead of the more common five and is slender with a narrow pointed head, ventral mouth and big eyes. It is similar to other species including the bluntnose sixgill shark and the frilled shark. The bigeye sixgill can be identified by the five teeth on each side of the lower jaw rather than the six of the bluntnose sixgill and by its ventral mouth as opposed to the frill shark's terminal mouth.

The frilled shark is one of the most primitive types of shark and little is known about its behaviour. Indeed, the only live specimen that has ever been captured was by staff from the Awashima Marine Park in Shizuoka, southwest of Tokyo, on 21 January 2007. They were alerted by fishermen to a "strange eel-like fish with razor sharp

teeth" that was later identified as a female 1.6m frilled shark. They removed it from the sea and put it into a salt water tank where they filmed and took pictures but unfortunately the shark died a few hours later. This rare surface appearance of a frilled shark has been attributed to the animal being unwell and possibly disoriented.

With a dark to light brown grey dorsal surface, lightening to a paler belly, the bignose sixgill shark has white trailing edges to its fins. It has fluorescent green eyes that help it see in the depths of the ocean where it lives on or near the bottom of warm temperate and tropical seas. They are deep water sharks, usually found offshore near the bottom to

BIGEYE SIXGILL SHARK

BIGEYE SIXGILL SHARK

depths of over 1,800 metres but it is believed they may rise towards the surface at night. Sightings do occasionally occur inshore, especially along rocky coasts or near islands, at depths of 25-50m but they are known to frequent continental and insular shelves and upper slopes with depths ranging from 90 metres to 600 metres.

Despite a wide distribution, the bigeye sixgill shark has only been reported in localised areas. They have been found in the western Atlantic Ocean off the coast of Mexico, the Bahamas, Cuba, Nicaragua and Costa Rica. On the opposite side of the Atlantic, sightings have been reported from France to Morocco as well as in the Mediterranean Sea. It is prevalent in the Indian Ocean – where it inhabits the waters of eastern and southern Africa – and the Pacific Ocean, including Australia, the Philippines and Japan.

The bigeye sixgill shark has been known to reach lengths of almost two metres and weigh 20kg, but the average size is just over one and a half metres. Males mature anywhere between 1.2-1.6m with females having to be slightly more developed at 1.4-1.7m. Although little has been researched on the mating habits and reproduction cycle of the bigeye sixgill shark, it is known that the species is ovoviviparous – eggs hatching within the mother shark – with litters of around 13 pups being born at approximately half a metre long.

They feed on a wide range of bony fish and other marine prey including chimeras, rays, squid, octopus, crabs, shrimps and even seals. They also scavenge on carrion and an immature tuna was found in the contents of one specimen's stomach, suggesting that they could feed nearer the surface than originally thought. Living as deep as it does, the bigeye sixgill shark has little to fear from man – other than being accidentally hooked on a long line or in trawls intended for other fish – and its only predators are presumed to be larger sharks.

With its small size and the fact that it lives in such deep waters, the bigeye sixgill shark is not considered a threat to divers and there have been no reported attacks. Although there is not enough information on this species to get a true picture of the density of the global population, the bigeye sixgill shark is not considered to be endangered. This is a reprieve for the species because it is estimated that it could take up to 14 years for the population numbers to double.

Chapter 5

Bignose Shark

THE BIGNOSE SHARK, CARCHARHINUS altimus, is a requiem shark of the family Carcharhinidae, with the genus name coming from the Greek karcharos meaning sharpen and rhinos meaning nose. It is also commonly called Knopp's shark and was first described in 1950 after a specimen was caught off the Florida Keys.

The bignose shark is a slender, cylindrical shark with a large, long, broad snout from which the name originates. It has long nasal flaps and high, triangular, saw-edged upper teeth. The inter-dorsal ridge is high and prominent, while the pectoral and dorsal fins are large and straight. The anal fin sits slightly further down the shark's body than the second dorsal fin. Similar to the night shark, the main difference in the two species is the second dorsal fin which differs in height and detail to the free rear tip. The bignose shark is also similar to but has a smaller snout than the sandbar shark, silky shark and dusky shark. It bears a resemblance to the blacktip shark and bull shark who lacks this species' inter-dorsal ridge.

The bignose shark is mainly grey with no conspicuous markings. It has a white underbelly and black tips on its pectoral fins and it can grow to a maximum size of three metres, weighing almost 170kg. They reach sexual maturity between approximately 2.1m (males) and 2.8m (females) and have a viviparous method of reproduction. After conception, the young are reared inside the mother with yolk sac placentas until they are born and emerge – with between two and 10 siblings – as mirror images of their parents at almost a metre long. As with many sharks, the timing of this depends on where in the world the sharks are living. In the Mediterranean Sea birth usually occurs between August and September, while off the coast of Africa in the Indian Ocean it is normally in September, or October around the island of Madagascar.

Bignose sharks can be found circumglobally in warm and tropical waters between latitudes 40°N and 34°S. They can be found in the Pacific Ocean around China, Hawaii, the Gulf of California, Mexico and Ecuador as well as in the Indian Ocean off Madagascar, South Africa, Mozambique and India. They are also at home in the Mediterranean Sea and the Atlantic, where they have been reported from Ghana to Senegal and from Florida to Venezuela.

Bignose sharks normally inhabit the

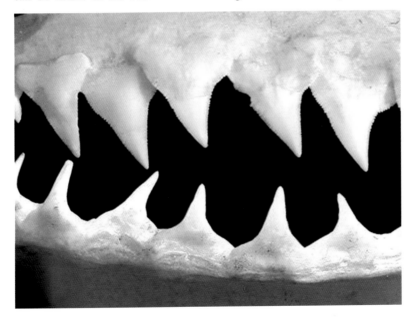

edge of the continental and insular shelves and uppermost slopes at depths of up to 400 metres. Sightings are rare in shallow waters. In fact, if you see one in shallow waters it is more likely to be a juvenile specimen as the adults prefer deeper water where they feed on bony fishes – including mackerel, sole and batfish – other sharks (such as cat sharks and dogfish), stingrays, and cuttlefish. Commercially fished by offshore trawlers, its flesh is utilised for fishmeal, its liver for the oil it contains, and the skin for shagreen. Shagreen is a type of roughened untanned leather, formerly made from a horse's back, but more commonly made from shark's skin since the 17th and 18th centuries. Such skins are naturally covered with placoid scales, with the size being dependent on the age and size of the shark – these scales are ground down to give a roughened surface. Shagreen is sometimes used for book bindings and small cases, as well as its more prevalent use to cover the handles of swords and daggers where slippery surfaces are not something you want to risk. It is currently illegal to fish commercially for the bignose shark in US waters and if caught the specimen must be released back into

the ocean in a way that ensures its best possible chance of survival. This practice is regulated by the National Marine Fisheries Service and it's hoped to minimise the number of accidental deaths.

Like the bigeye sixgill shark, there is little threat to humans from this creature of the deep and there have been no

reported attacks on humans. The bignose shark is commonly attacked by other sharks with the great white a confirmed adversary.

There is only one area of the world where there is sufficient information on the state of the ocean's bignose shark population and that is Australia. Here it is designated "Least Concern" by the World Conservation Union whereas in the rest of the world it is classified as "Data Deficient". Again, like the bigeye sixgill shark, if the bignose shark population does go into decline, then it is estimated that it will take the species more than 14 years to double its numbers.

Chapter 6

Blacktip Reef Shark

FOUND IN THE SHALLOW WATERS of the Caribbean and Indo-Pacific waters in temperatures of 20-27ºC is the blacktip reef shark. In Australia, the shark's range stretches between the central coasts of Western Australia and around the tropical north and south coasts, to southern Queensland. At times, this tropical shark will swim in waters as shallow as 30cm.

So named for the black tips on its pectoral and first dorsal fins, this small to medium sized shark is brown in colour on the top of its body, is usually whitish underneath and has a blunt and rounded snout. Running just below the first dorsal fin to above the ventral fin is a dark stripe, characteristic of this shark. Occasionally, the black tip of the dorsal fin has a white band below it. All other fins usually have a much smaller black tip.

Although some blacktip reef sharks have been measured up to six feet in length, they are usually not considered a real danger because of their generally small size. The average size for a blacktip reef shark is around 1.8 metres, although in the waters off Australia, the shark only reaches 1.4 metres.

Although not considered social, these sharks are often observed in small groups. With their oval eyes and cusped teeth, these sharks reach a maximum weight of 13.6kg and despite a preference for swimming in the shallows, are equally at home swimming at depths of 75 metres. Their natural habitat is in coral reefs and the inter-tidal zones or reef flats as well as near reef drops and mangrove areas. Blacktip reef sharks are also found in fresh water occasionally, but do not venture into tropical lakes or rivers far from the ocean. As one of the three most common reef

BLACKTIP REEF SHARK

sharks – along with the whitetip reef shark and the grey reef shark – in the Red Sea and East Africa to the Hawaiian Islands and the Tuamotu Archipelago, this shark is vulnerable to declining numbers in population.

Like all other sharks, the blacktip reef shark has no swim bladder and relies on its over-sized liver to keep it buoyant. Bony fish use a swim bladder for buoyancy which is a sac-like extension of the gut. Bubbles of gases can be introduced into it from the blood, or can be withdrawn. More bubbles make the whole fish lighter and less dense and so it is able to rise through the water, but the fish's control must be precise, as water pressure and the depth of the fish will affect the bubbles. With exactly the right buoyancy the bony fish can swim level and even seem to "hang".

Not so for the shark, who will sink to the bottom of the ocean floor if it stops swimming because its body mass is denser and heavier than water. Other aids which help the blacktip reef shark to keep from sinking are the intricate designs of the nose, tail and pectoral fins. While the tail moving in time with the shark moving at speed tends to push the nose down, the pectoral fins act like hydrofoils angled upwards helping to counter-balance the nose position, which greatly helps with buoyancy.

The female blacktip reef shark is viviparous and gives birth to living young that have been nurtured in the uterus by a placental sac. There are between two and four pups in a litter, born after a gestation period of around 16 months. Juveniles tend to measure between 33cm and 52cm at birth.

These sharks will feed on mullet and sturgeon although their main diet consists of reef fish. After birth, juveniles are typically found in extremely shallow water where they are more protected from larger predators. They are found swimming along the shoreline.

The blacktip reef shark is quite curious about scuba divers and snorkellers and is generally harmless unless threatened – in which case they form a sort of "S" shape with their bodies – or provoked. But the curiosity doesn't stop there. These sharks have been seen popping their heads out of the water to look around. They are also one of the very few sharks capable of breaching – where they leap fully out of the water.

Blacktip reef shark populations are steadily declining. Often caught accidentally in the nets of fishermen looking for other marine life and fish, these sharks are tossed aside after the catch has been hauled. However, in other areas, the populations of blacktip reef sharks are under threat from fishing where they are caught for their fins which are then used to make shark fin soup. In addition, the long gestation period combined with the small numbers of pups born in litters, means that the blacktip reef shark is not combative against its steady decline and struggles to replenish its populations.

Chapter 7

Blue Shark

THE BLUE SHARK, WITH ITS DIS-tinctive colouring, is instantly recognis-able. It is a deep indigo blue on top of its body and a bright vibrant blue on its sides with a whitish underside. The large pectoral fins are also a giveaway as they are as long out to the sides as they are between the tip of its pointed snout right down to the last gill slit.

Considered dangerous – and held responsible for many attacks on stricken ships and air disaster passengers – this formidable shark is long and slender, a fast swimmer that measures around 13 feet in length and weighs roughly between 60 and 80kg. Females tend to be slightly longer than males while the species as a whole is one of the most prevalent of all the large sharks.

With its large triangular serrated teeth in both the upper and lower jaws, the blue shark is a terrifying predator that inhabits deep water in tropical, sub-tropical and temperate oceans and seas worldwide. The shark's teeth are grouped in rows which can rotate into place as necessary. The first two rows are crucial for catching prey while the other rows enable the shark to keep a hold of the prey once caught.

Found in the Atlantic, Pacific and Indian Oceans in both inshore and offshore waters, the blue shark's range runs from the western Atlantic from Newfoundland to Argentina while its dominance as a major predator finds the species in abundance generally worldwide. In more temperate seas, the blue shark will venture closer to the shoreline while in tropical waters it tends to stay at much greater depths.

Blue sharks are known to migrate each year across the Atlantic Ocean eastward with the warm Gulf Stream. They migrate in a circle that follows the Caribbean Sea, along the US coast crossing to Europe before heading south to the African coast and back to the Caribbean Sea. The blue shark is often found in groups that are segregated by age and sex that reach as far north as Norway and as far south as Chile in South America.

Their diet – when not consuming the human variety – consists of squid, which is where its serrated teeth come in useful, sardines, anchovies and herring. They may even eat seals. Although blue sharks will eat flat fishes they prefer the pelagic bony fish including silver hake, white hake, red hake, cod, haddock, pollock, mackerel, tuna and swordfish. However, the blue shark is, like a number of other predators, an opportunistic feeder and will eat virtually anything it can including cuttlefish, octopus and blubber from whales and porpoise.

Renowned for being nomads, blue sharks are capable of swimming hundreds of miles each year. Considered one of the fastest sharks, they tend to gather in large groups. These pelagic, or open water, sharks gain exceptional power through their elongated tail fin which propels them swiftly through the water as it moves side to side. Some experts claim that the blue shark can swim at speeds of up to 60mph, although some scientists feel that this speed is greatly exaggerated and make more conservative estimates of 22mph. This is still an ongoing debate.

Females sexually mature around seven to 11 feet (at around five years old), while males typically mature at between six and nine feet. Courting involves the male biting the female and mature sharks are often sexed – accurately – by the presence or absence of scars. Female blue sharks have now adapted to survive the difficult mating ritual by developing a skin that is three times tougher than that of the male. It is possible for females to retain and nourish the spermatozoa in the oviducal gland for months or years while she waits to ovulate. After fertilisation, females give birth to between 25 and 50 pups after a gestation period lasting between nine and 12 months. These sharks are a viviparous species where females nurture the young in the uterus before giving birth to live pups. Pups are generally 16-20 inches in length at birth. The number of pups born to a litter, combined with the fact that they

have no predators of their own, have probably contributed to the fact that the blue shark is considered "Lower Risk" on the IUCN lists.

Often caught accidentally, the blue

shark is one of the most heavily-fished sharks there is and it is estimated that between 10 and 20 million sharks are killed in this manner each year. The meat of the blue shark is not highly sought after and most ends up as fishmeal. The skin is predominantly used for leather goods while the fins make shark fin soup. Like the basking shark, the blue shark's liver is sought after for its oil.

Chapter 8

Bluntnose SixGill Shark

ALSO KNOWN AS THE ATLANTIC mud shark, the brown shark and the bull dog shark, among many other names, the bluntnose sixgill shark is exactly what it says it is; a blunt nosed six gilled shark. Found in both temperate – meaning neither hot or cold – and tropical seas around the world this shark can be observed in the western Atlantic Ocean from North Carolina to Florida in the US and from the northern Gulf of Mexico to north Argentina. While in the eastern Atlantic, the bluntnose sixgill shark has a range that stretches from Iceland and Norway to south Namibia and the Mediterranean Sea. In the Indian Ocean, the shark moves between the coast of Madagascar and Mozambique and in the Pacific

Ocean it covers a range from the west including eastern Japan to Australia and New Zealand before stretching across to the waters off Hawaii.

This shark is mainly benthic – meaning deep water – and is often found resting on the bottom of the ocean during the day at depths of up to 6,500 feet. However, the shark is a predator and

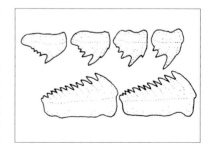

leaves the ocean bed to hunt nearer the surface at night. Despite little being known about the behaviour and migration of this shark – because it spends so much time at the bottom of the ocean – it has been mostly observed as solitary. The bluntnose sixgill shark is fairly prehistoric in appearance and from observation closely resembles shark fossils found from around 200 million years ago.

While its body is heavy and its head broad, the mouth is wide and rounded and its strange green "teardrop" eyes are located anterior to the mouth. With one dorsal fin that is found close to the tail fin (which is rather undeveloped for a shark), this large shark is capable of growing to 15.5 feet in length. The aver-age weight of a bluntnose sixgill shark is between 200kg (for a male) and 400kg (for a female). It is generally brown, grey or olive on top of its body while it is much paler underneath. Fins often have white markings. One of the shark's most distinguishing features is its six, saw-like teeth on each side of its lower jaw, while the upper jaw has nine smaller serrated teeth on each side. The bluntnose sixgill shark is often mistaken for the bigeyed sixgill shark and the frill shark.

Like all sharks, the bluntnose sixgill shark has a tough skin on

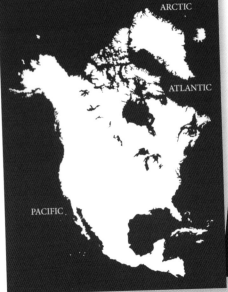

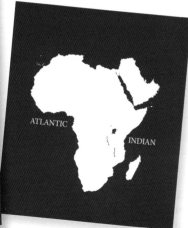

the exterior which hopefully deters would be predators. The skin is designed to contain highly sensitive organs which permit a carefully controlled exchange of water, salts and minerals between the sea water, body fluids and tissues within. The skin houses and supports an extraordinary system of muscles which are designed for power and control. These muscles have also cleverly evolved to ensure efficient energy consumption.

Female bluntnose sixgill sharks reach sexual maturity at around 18-35 years of age while males are estimated to reach maturity at 11-14 years. Reproduction is via ovoviparity and eggs hatch inside the female and thrive on nourishment gained from the yolk. After a long gestation a large litter of between 22 to more than a 100 juveniles are born. They tend to measure around 23-30 inches at birth.

Juveniles are left to fend for themselves and are seen swimming very close to shore. Life expectancy for this species is up to 80 years.

The bluntnose sixgill shark is fished commercially for its meat which is then marketed in a variety of ways including fresh. The shark is also used in oil production and as fishmeal and the fish is hunted recreationally. Bluntnose sixgills are also a product of by-catch. To catch this huge shark, fishermen use lines, traps, gillnets and trawls. The bluntnose sixgill shark has never been shown to become aggressive towards people unless provoked. The shark is curious and is not particularly bothered by scuba divers that come across it, however, it does not like to be surrounded or touched and will instantly head for deeper water if it feels in the slightest bit threatened.

Despite that, both commercial and recreational fishing of this shark is still allowed throughout the fish's range, it has become a "Near Threatened" species by the World Conservation Union. This union is a global institution made up of government agencies and non-government parties that assess the conservation and status of all living species. Currently, it is thought that the bluntnose sixgill shark is unable to maintain its populations against the pressures it faces from fishing and by-catch, however without proper monitoring worldwide and reliable statistics from which to work from, these claims are unsubstantiated.

Chapter 9

Bonnethead Shark

WITH ITS BONNET-SHAPED HEAD, the bonnethead shark is aptly named and it is thought that this strange head has become highly evolved in order to maximise the area where its sensory organs are located. The shark uses these sensors to detect physical, chemical and thermal changes in the water. In addition, the electrical fields that pass over these sensors enable the shark to accurately pinpoint its prey – including potential food that has buried itself on the ocean floor – such as crustaceans, rays and certain fish prone to hiding. It also eats octopus and molluscs. This evolutionary twist allows this particular shark, along with all hammerhead sharks, to search over larger areas for food at the bottom of the ocean than other shark species are able to do.

Although there is still much debate among experts as to why hammerheads have evolved completely in this way, it is known that the rounded shape of the head allows these types of species to swim on a horizontal plane and gives them the ability to turn sharply.

Due to scientific study it seems likely that the bonnethead shark is a quite recent development in sharks' evolutionary process.

The fins of this shark and other hammerhead species also differ from other shark species. In most other sharks, pectoral fins control the motion of the body up and down (pitching) and yawing – the side-to-side motion. These fins also control rolling. However, hammerhead species do not yaw or roll and achieve their up and down movements by using their heads. The bonnethead shark, because it is much smaller than other hammerheads, relies on both its head and its fins for pitching. This may

be the reason that its fins are larger and more developed than in other hammerheads. In addition, the bonnetheads are renowned for being the least buoyant of all sharks (along with other hammerheads) which means that they need to swim constantly, to keep the gills open and the water moving to maintain a steady supply of oxygen.

The bonnethead is a small and fairly common hammerhead shark whose eyes can be located at the edge of its rounded head. Its eyes have a tendency to shine due to the tapitial plate within that reflects light back into the lens. This is similar to shining a light in a cat's eyes and, like a cat, this particular shark also has a protective membrane (nictitating eyelid) that covers the eye during feeding. Coloured grey/brown, the bonnethead is, like many other sharks, lighter underneath. This shark grows to around three

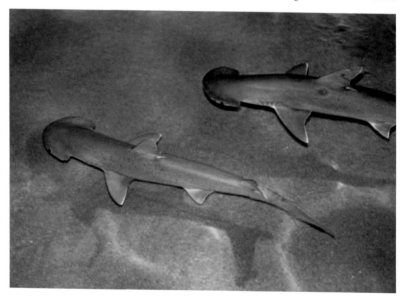

and a half feet long on average, although larger specimens are seen at around five feet and the average weight is 24lbs.

The range of the bonnethead shark is quite extensive and stretches from the sub-tropical waters in the western Atlantic from North Carolina to Brazil. While in the Caribbean Sea it can be found off the coast of Cuba and the Bahamas and into the Gulf of Mexico. In addition, this small timid shark can be observed in the eastern Pacific from southern California to Ecuador. Although rare, this shark has also been spotted off the coast of New England. Preferring the warmer waters of the world's oceans, bonnetheads like insular shelves near inshore coastal areas and can often be seen swimming along coral reefs and in the shallows of bays and estuaries. However, the bonnethead can swim to depths of around 80 metres.

Bonnethead sharks are social creatures and like to stay in groups of between five and 15 individuals. Sometimes they can be seen in schools of hundreds or even thousands, swimming continuously throughout their range. These sharks are likely to swim extremely long distances on a daily basis while they follow the changes in water temperature looking for the warmest spot.

The bonnethead shark is the only shark to show sexual dimorphism – whereby males and females can be recognised because they look different to one another. Male bonnetheads have a distinct bulge along the rounded head which becomes more pronounced with the onset of sexual maturity. Females in contrast have a more broadly rounded head. Bonnethead sharks are viviparous and the young are nurtured in the mother's uterus by a placental sac. It is not known in some of the shark's range whether mating takes place seasonally or all year round, although the most likely times for the bonnethead to mate are spring and autumn. In Brazil, mating definitely takes place in spring. Litters of between four and 16 pups are usual and juveniles usually measure around 12 inches at birth. Life expectancy is around 12 years.

As already mentioned these sharks are timid and therefore pose no particular threat to humans. Although global numbers of the bonnethead shark are not known, each population within its range is abundant and is not considered under threat, vulnerable or endangered.

Chapter 10

Bull Shark

THE BULL SHARK TAKES ITS NAME from its stout appearance and combative aggressive nature. It is also known as the Zambezi shark in Africa and the Ganges shark in India to name but a few. This heavy-bodied shark is extremely short by shark standards and has a broad, rounded snout. It has small eyes and a very large first dorsal fin. It is dark grey to pale grey in colour.

Bull sharks are found in a variety of ranges from tropical and sub-tropical coastal waters around the world, to rivers (some fresh water rivers) and lakes. These quarrelsome sharks have been observed more than 2,220 miles up the Amazon in Peru and over 1,800 miles up the Mississippi River in the US. The shark has also been found swimming up the Zambezi River in Africa – hence its alternative name. In Lake Nicaragua in Central America, a population of bull sharks were thought to be landlocked, however, it was later proved that they swam to the ocean through a maze of rivers and estuaries as it was

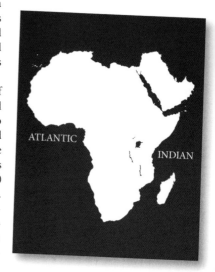

discovered that they are unable to remain in fresh water only.

The shark has a range which stretches from the western Atlantic coast off Massachusetts to Brazil and the Gulf of Mexico and from the Caribbean Sea to the Bahamas. In the eastern Atlantic it is found from Morocco to Angola. In the Indian Ocean it ranges west to South Africa, Iraq and India, while the range stretches east in the western Pacific to Thailand, Vietnam, Australia and the Philippines. It is also found in the eastern Pacific from California to Ecuador. The bull shark will head further north in its range during the summer months but will return to warmer waters in tropical climes during the winter.

Bull sharks are typical of many predators and are opportunistic feeders that will eat just about anything. They particularly enjoy bony fish, rays, sea turtles, dolphins, birds, other sharks and, on occasion, other bull sharks. Other food typically includes catfish and mackerel as well as crabs and squid. Bull sharks appear slow swimmers while on the look out for prey but they can move quickly if they need to and have been clocked at more than 11mph.

Female bull sharks are slightly larger than males and measure eight feet on average and weigh about 285lbs. Males average at around seven feet with an average weight of roughly 209lbs. Females also have a longer life span at 16 years compared to 12 years for males. Mating takes place all year round in most of the shark's range. Breeding does occur in fresh water although it does

not take place as often as it does in the coastal areas of the shark's habitat. Bull sharks are viviparous and the juveniles benefit from a placental sac in the female's uterus. Gestation is between 10 and 11 months and litters commonly produce between four and 13 pups. Each pup is around 55cm to 80cm at birth however their growth rate is particularly slow – even for sharks – and this makes them a target for adult bull sharks in shallow waters. Other than this they have very few natural predators, except perhaps tiger sharks and sandbar sharks. However, a crocodile was allegedly responsible for eating a

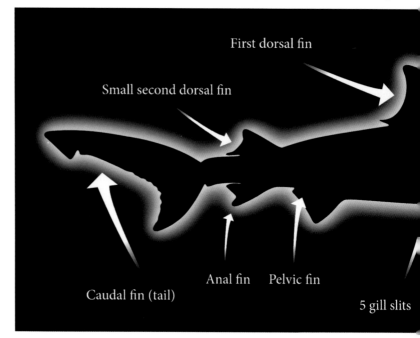

First dorsal fin

Small second dorsal fin

Anal fin   Pelvic fin

Caudal fin (tail)

5 gill slits

whole bull shark in South Africa.

The shark itself is not a major target for commercial fishing but long lines used by fishermen are often a problem for bull shark populations when they are caught as by-catch. However, from the little commercial fishing of these sharks that does take place, populations are in decline. The skin is used in leather goods while fins are the delicacy of shark fin soup. Recreationally, the bull shark is a popular game fish, particularly in the US and South Africa. The shark is not legally protected in any part of its range, although the population around the coast of South Africa does appear to be in decline according to reports. On the IUCN list, the bull shark is currently labelled "Near Threatened" but is not yet considered vulnerable or endangered.

Bull sharks are capable of unprovoked attacks on humans. According to records, this particular species of shark is responsible for around 70 attacks on humans worldwide, 17 of which were fatal. However, this fairly low figure is probably unrepresentative of the actual numbers of attacks and fatalities in reality when the close proximity of their activities to humans is considered. In areas such as Mexico, India, South America, the Middle East and some parts of Asia, attacks go unreported and records are often sketchy. Experts believe that the actual figures are much higher than documented. Some experts even go so far as to claim that the bull shark is the most dangerous shark in the world.

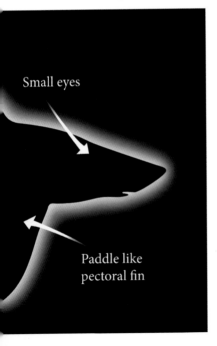

Small eyes

Paddle like pectoral fin

Chapter 11

Cookie Cutter Shark

NAMED FOR THE STYLE IN WHICH it eats, the cookie cutter shark creates "cookie cutter" bites in the skin of other sharks and large marine animals. Also known as the cigar shark – for its cigar-shaped body – and the luminous shark, this particularly aggressive species of shark is a small, elusive, dogfish shark.

It has two very small spineless dorsal fins where the first dorsal fin is located in front of the pelvic fins. With its large eyes positioned to the front of the head and bulbous snout, it is dark brown and lighter below and has a dark collar around the gill region. Growing up to 20 inches in length, the cookie cutter has a bio-luminous underside that glows green and pale blue-green against the background light of the ocean's surface. This serves as the shark's camouflage to the creatures swimming beneath it. In addition, one small patch appears to be black which is a mechanism for deceiving prey by making the cookie cutter look smaller than it really is.

Many marine predators swim in deeper waters looking above for the dark silhouettes of smaller prey which they can attack. Smaller predatory fish, such as tuna, thinking that the cookie cutter is a smaller fish will attack. When they do, the cookie cutter attacks back and catches itself another meal. The cookie cutter is also partial to squid. The cookie cutter shark is the only marine animal or fish known to have this effective form of camouflage and disguise. There are no other instances where a bio-luminescent lure is created without the aid of a luminescence. The ability of this shark to produce this belly adaptation is called counter-illumination. This glow is produced by thousands of tiny photophores packed tightly together.

The cookie cutter shark is found worldwide in tropical oceans and seas. It ranges from the western Atlantic (in the Bahamas) to southern Brazil and travels through southern Angola to South Africa. It also ranges over to Mauritius and New Guinea to Western Australia before heading around Queensland, New South Wales and Tasmania. It then ranges north to Japan and then travels as far as Hawaii and the Galapagos Islands. Despite this wide

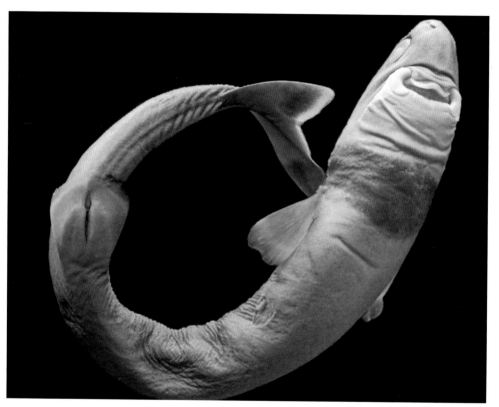

range, the cookie cutter is fairly scattered around the globe.

This shark is renowned for taking bite-sized chunks out of the flesh of whales and larger sharks as well as dolphins, marlins and the megamouth shark. Although it is not known for sure, scientists believe that this shark rotates itself around once it has a hold of the larger fish or mammal in order to achieve its highly symmetrical cut. It has been suggested that because the cookie cutter appears smaller than it actually is, when the larger predator comes to attack the small shark the forward movement of the fish or mammal gives the shark more leverage to secure a good grip with its teeth.

The teeth of the cookie cutter are strong and erect in the upper jaw and triangular in the lower jaw and both upper and lower are saw-like. Its succour-like lips enable the shark to latch on to larger animals where they create an oral vacuum. For this reason, the cookie cutter is considered a parasite. As well as living like a shark the cookie cutter also lives like an ectoparasite where it lives off the flesh of another living organism. The victim is left badly – although neatly – scarred, but alive.

The cookie cutter is a benthic shark – meaning deep water – and spends the majority of its time in depths of up to 3,300 feet below the surface of the ocean. During vertical migration however the cookie cutter is known to come to the surface at night in search of prey.

There is very little known about the reproduction of the cookie cutter shark – probably because it is such a deep ocean shark – however, it is known that it is viviparous and so does not lay eggs. Each embryo is nurtured by a placental sac within the female's uterus. They are then born as live young rather than hatchlings. The litter usually consists of around six or seven pups.

There has been very little interaction between the cookie cutter and humans which is probably due to the shark's benthic nature. However, there have been several attacks on submarines by cookie cutter sharks. It is thought that rather than attacking the submarine per se, the cookie cutter has mistakenly taken the fast moving vessel for larger prey.

The large-tooth cookie cutter shark is shaped the same way as the cookie cutter shark and like its close cousin has two spineless dorsal fins. However, it has a huge row of 19 teeth – which proportionally are the largest teeth found in any shark species – in its lower jaw. Like the cookie cutter, the large-tooth cookie cutter grows to around 20 inches and is also a parasite, living off the flesh of other marine life, particularly larger species.

Chapter 12

Dogfish Shark

THE DOGFISH SHARK WAS OFFI-cially named in 1758 and is known by other names including blue dog, common spinyfish, spiny dogfish, Pacific

dogfish and spiky dog. With their grey/slate brown colouring and pale white belly these sharks are easily distinguished from other small sharks by a row of small white dots running along their sides. However, some older dogfish sharks tend to lose the white spots in later life. The dogfish shark has a slender body while its head tends to slope towards its blunt snout.

Males are usually smaller than females who can reach up to three and a half feet in length and weigh a healthy eight pounds. Like its cousin the smooth dogfish, the dogfish shark possesses flat grinding teeth, however it also has a set of very sharp teeth. There are 28 teeth in the upper jaw and 24 teeth in the lower jaw. The spine of the dogfish shark shows growth zones allowing the fish to be aged. The oldest documented dogfish shark was around

25-30 years old. Despite their size, these small sharks are renowned for being voracious eaters and prey on a large variety of marine life including shrimp, crab, squid and numerous types of bony fish. They are also opportunistic predators and will eat virtually anything. If threatened, the dogfish shark will use its spines in defence by curling itself around – the spines are believed to be mildly poisonous. They travel in large groups or schools of sharks equal to their size and are usually found at a depth of around 2,950 feet. Schools

can consist of mature females, mature males, immature females or juvenile sharks of both sexes. Groups of dogfish sharks can number from hundreds to thousands of individuals. Some dogfish sharks do, however, prefer to remain solitary.

Common both inshore and offshore, the dogfish shark prefers temperate and sub-arctic water. It is found in the western Atlantic Ocean with a range from Greenland to Argentina while in the eastern Atlantic it is observed from Iceland to Russia and South Africa, the Black Sea and Mediterranean Sea. In the Pacific Ocean it is found from the Bering Sea to New Zealand and in the eastern Pacific from the Bering Sea to Chile. They are primarily a benthic shark, but like the cookie cutter, they migrate upwards to the surface. They prefer sea water but can sometimes be found in slightly less salty brackish water, however, they are unable to tol-

DOGFISH SHARK

erate fresh water. Dogfish sharks are known for being highly migratory and for example, in the Atlantic travel from Cape Cod during the summer months, south to Long Island during the autumn to as far south as North Carolina in winter. The migration north begins in the spring.

Females mature at about 12 years of age, while males mature age six. Mating usually takes place offshore and reproduction is ovoviviparous. The dogfish shark is thought to have the longest gestation of any shark species at around 24 months. Each juvenile is born with sheaths over its spines to stop it from injuring its mother. There are usually six or seven pups in a litter and they are often between eight and 13 inches long at birth.

Where the dogfish shark population is abundant in the mid-Atlantic, they are considered a pest by commercial and game fishermen. Due to their large appetites, the dogfish sharks drive off mackerel and herring while trying to eat them, which becomes highly disruptive for the commercial fisheries. They will even bite through the fishing nets to get to the catch, releasing many of the fish in the process. They are renowned for

following – attacking and eating – the schools of herring that are returning to the coastal waters of British Columbia. As this is the time that fishing of the more commercially acceptable herring is taking place, the dogfish sharks are renowned for plugging nets in their attempt to catch the fish before the fishermen. This does not make the shark popular. However, in some European countries, the meat is considered a delicacy.

Dogfish sharks themselves are preyed on by whales, larger species of sharks, goosefish and cod. Their populations were at a peak during the 1970s, but declined during the following decade. By the 1990s their numbers were in sharp decline.

They pose little threat to humans, but fishermen who land dogfish sharks as by-catch are mindful of their spiny dorsal fins. The shark is vulnerable to over-fishing which is not helped by their long gestation period, small litters and slow growth. Under the IUCN, the dogfish shark is considered at low risk and appears as "Near Threatened" on the union's list in most of its range. But, it has been assessed as vulnerable and endangered in the northwest and northeast Atlantic as a result of over-fishing. However, despite all this, the dogfish shark is fairly abundant off the coast of Alaska and is the most prevalent shark in the region.

Chapter 13

Galapagos Shark

THIS LARGE SHARK IS AN AGGRESsive species named when specimens were first found near the Galapagos Islands in the Pacific Ocean off the coast of Ecuador in 1905. The Galapagos shark is also known as the grey reef whaler and mackerel shark.

With its slender muscular body which is tapered at both ends, the Galapagos has a broad, rounded snout and looks extremely similar to the grey reef shark and the dusky shark. But, the Galapagos shark can be distinguished by its pointed straight dorsal fin and larger teeth. Its body is a grey/brown colour and it has a whitish underside. In some Galapagos sharks the fins show dusky markings while others may have a white band-like marking around the flanks. This shark has particularly sharp teeth and the lower jaw has finely serrated teeth which stand erect. The upper jaw also has serrated teeth, but these are relatively long and triangular in shape. The Galapagos shark on average reaches around 10 feet, however, it is possible for the shark to measure more than 12 feet.

True distribution is difficult to determine given that there are a number of shark species that closely resemble the Galapagos shark. But it is renowned for keeping close to and remaining prevalent in the tropical waters surrounding oceanic islands. The Galapagos is very rarely solitary and groups or schools of the species are found in the Indian Ocean. Here, the shark is found in the waters south of Madagascar while in the Pacific Ocean it is known to live off the coast of Hawaii, Galapagos and the Îles Tuamotu Archipelago, also known as the island group of French Polynesia in the central South Pacific Ocean. It is also found in the Atlantic around

Bermuda and the Virgin Islands as well as Cape Verde and Saint Helena.

It is a pelagic – open water – shark that is typically found inshore and occasionally offshore around insular shelves at a depth of around 591 feet for feeding, but the range can be anywhere between 20 feet and 200 feet at other times. Juveniles, however, are more likely to be limited to around 82 feet. This more shallow depth helps to act as a nursery ground and protects the sharks to some extent from being eaten by their own species. The shark is known to prefer waters with strong currents that move quickly over corals or rocky ocean beds. In the Îles Tuamotu there are 75 atolls – a type of low coral

island – that are joined by innumerable coral reefs. Around these particular islands and atolls, the Galapagos sharks enjoy a double chain of reefs which stretch for roughly 900 miles. But, despite being considered a coastal species, the Galapagos has been spotted swimming across open waters between islands.

As a benthic feeding – deep water – shark, the Galapagos is found feeding from the ocean floor. Its primary diet consists of bottom-dwelling fishes, squid and octopus, although it will also eat eels, flatheads, groupers, flatfish and triggerfish. There are also reports that in certain ranges the shark will feed on sea lions – and it will eat its own young.

Galapagos sharks mate for the first time at around 10 years old in both males and females when the male is typically around seven to seven and a half feet while the female sexually matures at around seven to eight feet in length. Mating takes place early in the year and it is renowned for being a fairly aggressive act. Females are typically covered in bite marks and scars around their gills, fins and body where they have been bitten by the male. Galapagos sharks are viviparous and give birth to live young rather than laying eggs. The embryo is nourished by a placental sac in the mother's uterus during gestation. A litter of between four and 16 pups is usual with each pup measuring around 24-30 inches at birth. Life expectancy of the Galapagos shark is around 25 years.

These sharks are a danger to humans and attacks are fairly common. Like many other species of sharks, Galapagos sharks are quite inquisitive and are known to follow divers. It has been reported that when they become a hindrance, divers who have taken aggressive action to deter the sharks don't get rid of them, but merely excite the sharks more. If the shark itself wants to display a threatening posture it will arch its back, raise its head and swim in a twisted and rolling motion. There has been one official recorded fatality in the Virgin Islands where a Galapagos attacked a human.

Despite just one death, the shark is still considered dangerous to man and it is advisable to limit your movement in the water if one of the shark's regular food sources is present or if the school of Galapagos sharks is quite large. On the IUCN list the shark is considered "Near Threatened" but has little commercial value.

Chapter 14

Goblin Shark

WITH ITS LONG, FLAT, POINTED snout, the goblin shark is a rare fish which is extremely unusual to look at. Sometimes referred to as the elfin shark, it is thought that its long snout may contain electro-sensory canals which help the shark to locate its prey. Another unusual feature of this strange, prehistoric looking shark is its mouth – containing 26 teeth in the upper jaw and 24 in the lower which all appear fang-like – which can protrude forward under the snout or can be retracted to a position under its eyes.

Aside from its two peculiar attributes, the Goblin shark is basically the same as many other species in that it is uniform with its five gills and two dorsal fins. The dorsal fins are small and contain no spines and remain low and rounded to the shark's body. The anal fin is larger while the pectoral fins are small. The pelvic fins are larger than the dorsal fins. It has a fairly flabby body and a tail that sports a weak lower lobe. The shark's colouration is grey/pink and paler on the underside and a typical example can grow up to 14 feet. The pink colouration – which is unique among sharks – is caused by blood vessels underneath its semi-transparent skin. The skin bruises easily and causes the colouring.

However, this shark is rarely seen. It is thought to be a slow swimmer. It is not understood why the shark's liver is extremely large – in some cases weighing up to 25% of the shark's body weight. The shark has long, smooth-edged front teeth while the rear teeth are designed for crushing prey. Scientists have yet to establish the true picture of this remarkable fish however they do know that it is the only surviving member of the "Mitsukurina" family, which were identified from fossils. All other species are now extinct.

There are very few specimens of the goblin shark that have been scientifically recorded. The goblin shark was first caught off the coast of Yokohama in the "Black Current" by Japanese fishermen in 1898. The fishermen called the strange fish "tenguzame" meaning goblin. Found mostly off the coast of Japan at depths of up to 1,200 metres, the shark is benthic and prefers the safety of the ocean floor. Also found throughout the Pacific, Atlantic and Indian Oceans around the coast of Australia – particularly New South Wales, Tasmania and possibly South Australia – the shark is

GOBLIN SHARK

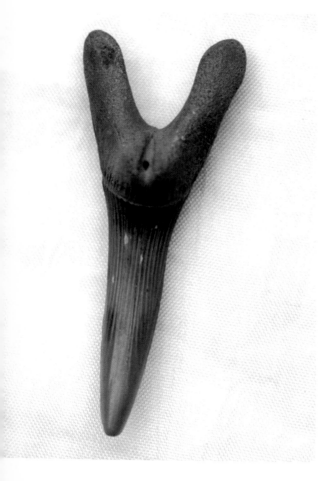

not considered dangerous to humans. In the western Atlantic, the goblin shark can be found around the coast of French Guiana while in the east it is native to the Bay of Biscay, Madeira and Portugal. It also has a range in the waters off South Africa. Its distribution is thought to be wide and recent sightings have included the shark being spotted off the coast of California and the northern Gulf of Mexico just south of Mississippi.

The typical diet of the goblin shark is rockfish – a deep sea spiny fish – octopus and crab. By using its elongated snout, it is believed that the shark can sense its prey and will shoot out its jaws to catch the prey in its teeth. It has also developed a sucking motion to enable it to catch its prey more effectively. Very little else is known about its feeding habits and the shape of its teeth suggest that it is more inclined to eat soft prey but this has not been substantiated. However, the shark is known to suffer from a number of parasites including tapeworms.

Goblin sharks are thought to be ovoviviparous and give birth to live pups once the eggs have hatched inside the female. But this has never been

proved as no pregnant females have ever been caught.

Fisheries and fishermen do not see much commercial value in the goblin shark and it is usually only caught by accident in by-catch of deep water trawls and gill nets. It is possible to dry and salt the fish for human consumption.

Sadly, it seems as if little will be known about this shark for some time to come as serious research costs a great deal of money. In addition, the money needed for research is usually only found if the research may lead to useful projects and guaranteed profit. Academic research into sharks for the sake of it is a difficult funding issue and shark scientists work mainly in three areas including studying the biology and ecology of commercially fished sharks, developing shark products and finding shark deterrents.

The shark rarely comes into contact with humans but considering its large size it is thought to be a potential threat. The shark is not listed on the IUCN list of endangered, threatened or vulnerable species.

Chapter 15

Great White Shark

RENOWNED FOR BEING ONE OF the most feared of all the ocean's predators, the great white has a ferocious reputation as a killer. As a pelagic – open water – shark, this massive fish is found in the coastal surface waters of all the earth's major oceans. Capable of reaching lengths of up to 20 feet, the great white can weigh up to 4,500lbs and is the only known surviving species of its family "Carcharodon". Average sizes however, record males at around 15 feet weighing around 2,500lbs while females are slightly larger. Despite our fears of this shark, humans are its only real threat, although killer whales have been known to attack and prey on great whites.

The snout is large and conical-shaped and it is coloured grey with a white underside. Unlike most other sharks, the great white has the same sized lobes on the upper and lower side of the tail fin and has unattached teeth within the jaw which are retractable. These move into place when the shark's mouth opens and are highly sensitive. They are also serrated and act like a saw when the shark moves its head powerfully from side to side allowing it to take huge chunks off the prey. Like the blacktip reef sharks, great whites are regularly found popping their heads above the surface of the water – this is known as "spy-hopping".

Great whites have the ability, by using their specially designed "sixth sense", to locate movement in the water of other living species. Their diet consists primarily of small sharks, turtles, dolphins, seals, sea lions, fish and occasionally stingrays – this includes the sting as well. They also eat items that cannot be digested along with the occasional human. Using the electro-sensory

device common to sharks the great white is able to locate prey from a fair distance away. Once near enough, the shark will then use its smell and hearing to establish that it has found prey, while its eyes will enable it to attack.

Great whites are an ambush predator and like many other larger sharks swim below the prey aiming to surprise attack. Scientists have been able to establish that hunting takes place early in the morning and that attack rates drop substantially by late morning. The great white is a powerful shark capable of great speed and some have been known to actually launch themselves out of the water when hunting and chasing a seal or sea lion. Along with the

spinner shark, basking shark and por-beagle among others, the great white is one of the few sharks that can jump fully out of the water. Hunting involves the shark taking a huge bite of the prey then backing off. This avoids a counter-attack by forceful opponents (including sea lions) before the shark ventures back to the prey. Common in the offshore waters of the globe, the great white has greater populations off the southern coast of Australia, South Africa, California and Mexico. To a lesser extent it is also prevalent in the Mediterranean and Adriatic Seas as well as the tropical waters off the coast of the Caribbean and Mauritius.

The mating habits of the great white have not been fully observed, however, the shark is ovoviviparous and females hatch their eggs inside before giving birth to live pups. Males are typically around 12 feet when they sexually mature while females are around 15 feet. Litters typically include seven to nine young who are fully functioning predators when they leave their mother's body. Life expectancy of the great white is unknown however some experts believe that a life span of around 30-40 years is fairly accurate.

Despite attacks on humans by great whites, their reputation as man eaters

is unfair. Most shark attacks happen in error – it's a case of mistaken identity – and it is believed that they sometimes bite out of curiosity. Most attacks are stopped when companions of the victim rescue them by getting them out of the water quickly.

Solo divers with no back-up are most at risk. Human flesh, bone, and fat are actually not good for the shark's digestive system and many divers and surfers use a POD (electronic beacon) which disturbs the shark's own sensory organs hopefully avoiding attack. However, vicious attacks do happen and in Australia in 1985 a mother of four was attacked in seven feet of water. The first bite saw the woman bitten in half. Rescuers were faced with a headless torso which the great white returned for before it could

be recovered from the sea.

Great white populations have been declining since the 1970s and the fish is now considered endangered on the IUCN list. The increase in fishing – for the shark's jaws, fins, teeth and for game – for great whites seems the most likely culprit in their demise but actual numbers of populations in the various ranges worldwide are not known. Our fascination – and tourism – grows in the great white probably because its one of the few fish that can actually eat humans alive – and sometimes does.

Chapter 16

Greenland Shark

THE ARCTIC OCEAN IS A DIFFICULT environment for the Greenland shark with its formidable ice and snow. Plunged into darkness during the winter months, it is buffeted by blizzards and cold. Life in the Arctic means enduring some of the most extremes in temperature known on the planet, yet marine life is possible and the Greenland shark thrives in these cold dark hostile waters. Summer time is the only real chance that experts have to study the environment and observations are compromised by the lack of scientific study during the winter months. This is a particular concern at the moment as the ecosystem appears increasingly vulnerable.

Despite its harsh habitat, the Greenland shark is a particularly large species capable of reaching up to 24 feet in length. Growth, however, is slow due to the extreme cold climate in which it lives. With an average weight of 2,250 lbs the Greenland shark is fished commercially around the waters of Greenland. Other names for this huge shark include the sleeper shark, gurry shark, ground shark or grey shark. However, very little is actually known about this mammoth shark and it does not enjoy the kind of fame or publicity that the great white does.

Renowned for its sluggish and fairly inactive approach to life, the Greenland shark is the largest Arctic fish but its razor-like teeth are small. It is not as aggressive as other large sharks and has a problem with blindness, often caused by parasites – copepods – which hang on to the shark's eyes. These pink/white parasites attach themselves to the shark's cornea, living off the corneal tissue, and scientists and experts are unde-

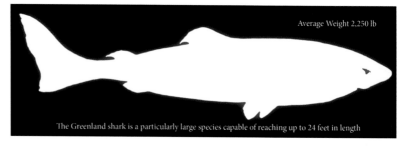

Average Weight 2,250 lb

The Greenland shark is a particularly large species capable of reaching up to 24 feet in length

cided as to why this should be the case. Some argue that the dangling parasites are used by the shark to attract food – Greenland sharks are able to inhale and suck food into their mouths from a distance of three feet. Its colouration is dark brown and its flesh is poisonous to many other animals and contains a harmful toxin. It has a short broad tail which is ideal for accelerating, leading some experts to question the shark's renowned slow movements, however, this has not yet been proved either way. Noticeable for its small gills in relation to its size, the Greenland has no spines in its dorsal fins.

As an arctic fish, the Greenland lives further north than any other species of shark in the waters of the north Atlantic Ocean around Greenland and Iceland. Greenland sharks are benthic – deep water – sharks and often live at depths of up to 2,000 metres (deeper than other sharks) feeding mainly on spiny fish and mammals such as seals. Living mainly along the coast of Greenland and the fjords, the Greenland shark is also known to occupy the Arctic Ocean year round and will travel as far as the Gulf of St Lawrence. It has repeatedly been found washed ashore in the Saguenay Fjord since 1888. Sharks leaving their native habitat have also been spotted as far east as Portugal and France and having reached the Gulf of St Lawrence, have also been reported to have moved as far south as Cape Cod and North Carolina. The Greenland has also been spotted in the south of the Atlantic Ocean off the coast of Argentina as well as the Antarctic.

Although the shark feeds mainly on

fish and seals, other interesting animals have been found in the stomachs of Greenland sharks including parts of polar bears, horses and reindeer. However, the shark's more usual dietary supplements include squid, herring, salmon and narwhal – a type of whale – and the beluga or white whale, which is closely related to the narwhal.

Inuit hunters catch the Greenland by luring the shark to a chopped hole in the ice. It is then either harpooned or dragged out of the water by hand. Despite its toxic flesh, if prepared correctly it is possible to eat the Greenland shark. The toxin when digested breaks down in the body producing a reaction similar to intoxication from alcohol. However, if the shark is boiled in many changes of water or is dried or exposed to freezing and thawing in the ground it is possible to eat the flesh safely and in parts of Greenland and Iceland it is considered a delicacy. When the sharks are caught by hunters, or accidentally washed ashore, the meat – when dried – is fed to dogs while Eskimos use the skin for leather items including boots and teeth are used as knives. In addition, the shark is fished by Greenland, Iceland and Norwegian fishermen for its liver oil. Although informa-tion on actual numbers is difficult to gauge, populations are thought to be relatively low at this time. This shark is ovo-viviparous and the females lay eggs before giving birth to live young. There is only one documented report of an attack on a human by a Greenland shark which took place in Canada in 1859. Details of the event are sketchy and its authenticity was never proven.

Chapter 17

Hammerhead Shark

THESE AGGRESSIVE PREDATORS are members of the Sphyrnidae family and have – as the name suggests – a hammer-like head which has been found to make the shark negatively buoyant. The head is indented at the centre of the hammer-shape which is almost rectangular. Some experts believe the hammerheads to be more highly evolved than other shark species and that the wide separation of their eyes gives superior vision. Most of the sharp turns and moves the hammerhead makes are controlled and executed by its specially designed vertebrae rather than the shape of its head as was once thought.

They have a small mouth which is designed to achieve maximum affect when hunting for prey on the bottom of the ocean. Their teeth are triangular and deeply serrated on the edges. Although solo hunters at night, the scalloped hammerhead is known to join groups of other hammerheads during the day. Sometimes these schools are large and may consist of hundreds of individuals. It is thought that the schools of hammerheads are formed around both feeding and reproduction habits.

Some experts believe that groups of sharks stay together for increased protection, but this is questioned by others who point out that the hammerhead sharks have no predators of their own once they reach maturity. When scalloped hammerhead's are grouped together smaller numbers will break away to swim to shallower water where angel fish and wrasse will peck at their skin to clean them. The great hammerhead is a solitary creature and hunts along the sea bed in search of its prey.

There are nine species of hammer-

HAMMERHEAD SHARK

head sharks and they range from six and a half feet up to nearly 20 feet in length. The average weight of a hammerhead shark is around 500lbs, but some have been found to weigh in excess of 1,000lbs. All these species have the same hammer-type head with eyes and nostrils positioned at the tips of the flattened extensions to the side. Coloured from olive to light brown, hammerhead's have a second dorsal fin which almost reaches the tail fin. Fins are typically darker in juveniles but grow lighter as the shark ages.

Found typically in tropical and subtropical waters along coastlines globally, the hammerhead lives on the continental shelves and reaches depths of around 260 feet in the world's oceans. Some populations of hammerheads remain in familiar waters while others are migratory at certain times of the year.

The great hammerhead is known to migrate seasonally in search of cooler waters during the summer months. Some sexually related migrations have also been recorded and female scalloped hammerheads are known to migrate during particular periods of their sexual development. It is known that migrating hammerheads make use of the earth's magnetic field. Smooth hammerheads prefer shallow coastal waters migrating north in the summer to cooler climes and returning south during the winter months.

Its exceptional sense of smell through its large nasal tracts is probably the most efficient way for a hammerhead to find prey however its ability to detect prey with its electro-sensory skills is astounding. The sensory receptors are spread over a wide area and it is recorded that a hammerhead can detect an electrical signal of half a billionth of a volt. The shark's primary diet consists of spiny fish, smaller sharks, such as the Atlantic sharpnose shark and the blacktip reef shark, squid, octopus, lobster and crab although the hammerhead is known to be cannibalistic with smaller members of its own species. Other favoured prey includes sardines, herring and mackerel. A particular favourite in the hammerheads diet is the stingray which it pins down before devouring the ray's wings.

Like other large predators, mating is a violent affair and male scalloped hammerheads bite the females into submission to allow mating to occur. Like other shark species, fertilisation is internal and the hammerhead is viviparous.

The embryos are fed by the placental sac during gestation which typically lasts between 10 and 12 months. Litters usually consist of between 20 and 40 pups. The cartilage in the hammer-shaped head of the live young is soft to allow an easier birth. The pups are around 70cm at birth and once born are left by the mother to fend for themselves as is typical in all sharks. The great hammerhead is also viviparous and produces a litter of between 15 and 40 pups. It has been suggested that large schools of scalloped hammerheads are formed around mating rituals where females manoeuvre for position in the middle, with the larger females occupying prime positions. This makes them more dominant and more attractive to males.

On the whole, hammerhead sharks are relatively harmless to humans however some species including the great hammerhead are considered a threat. Most attacks on humans seem to take place by accident or happen as a result of the shark being surprised, threatened or provoked in some way. There have been roughly around 40 attacks with just less than half of these being unprovoked attacks.

Chapter 18

Lemon Shark

THE LEMON SHARK HAS BEEN SCI-entifically well studied and a great deal more is known about this particular shark than many others. The reason for this is partly because the shark survives well in captivity whereas many others do not. Many sharks in captivity refuse food and die fairly quickly after capture. Much is known about the nature and ecology of the lemon shark and the population based around the Bimini Islands off the coast of the western Bahamas, is probably one of the most studied populations of all shark species.

Belonging to the Carcharhinidae family, the lemon shark was first documented in 1868 and began appearing in literature around 1882. The shark gets its name from its deep yellow/brown colouration on its back, although like many sharks it is lighter underneath. It is a fairly large stocky fish with a blunt snout and two dorsal fins of a similar size. The lemon shark's teeth are finely serrated and narrow and are long and thin designed to catch slippery fish – the staple diet. Both sexes reach sexual maturity around seven years of age and typically the shark grows to an average length of around eight to 10 feet and has a growth rate of 21 inches per year.

The lemon shark is found in the Atlantic off Africa, the Gulf of Mexico and South America as well as in the eastern Pacific Ocean off South America along the coast as far as California. This species is particularly prevalent in the Caribbean. The shark will swim in the ocean during migration, but typically stays along continental and insular shelves of the sub-tropical shallows where it reaches a depth of up to 300 feet. It prefers coral reefs, enclosed bays, river mouths and mangroves, but does

not swim far into fresh waters. The shark is pelagic and prefers the open water where groups of lemon sharks are found on the water's surface during the day although they will reach deeper waters at night. Most populations of lemon shark have a range of 18-92 square kilometres. Groups of schools of lemon sharks have been recently monitored off the coast of Florida.

The meetings are seasonal and have surprised experts.

The majority of the lemon shark's diet consists of stingrays, catfish, mullet, jacks, porcupine fish, guitarfish, crayfish and crabs, although the shark will also eat birds, molluscs and smaller sharks.

Mating takes place in shallow waters during the spring. The lemon shark is viviparous and embryos are nurtured by

a placental sac rather than being laid as eggs across the ocean floor. Gestation is typically between 10 and 12 months and females swim to shallow nursery grounds during April and September to give birth to live young. The lemon shark's typical litter size is around four to 16 pups which measure around 20 inches at birth. It is thought that females will wait 12 months before reproducing again. Juveniles are known to lose a full set of teeth every week or so. The first two rows of teeth are used to catch and hold on to prey while subsequent teeth can be rotated into place as necessary. Juveniles stay in shallow water for protection from larger sharks for several years. They can also stand lower or higher levels of salt water than adults and can even swim in fresh water. Their main diet consists of fishes that primarily live in mangroves although one fifth of their diet is made up of invertebrates.

The shark is fished commercially as well as for game along the Atlantic Ocean off the coast of the US, the Caribbean and the Pacific Ocean. Like many other species of shark, the lemon shark is also caught as by-catch. The skin is sought after for leather goods while the meat is popular. However, the main reason for catching these sharks is for their highly prized fins which are exported to Asia to make shark fin soup. Populations in some areas, including the Pacific Ocean and the western north Atlantic, are in decline due to over-fishing. Lemon sharks in the Atlantic off the coast of the US are currently managed by the National Marine Fisheries Service who monitor the fish through a quota and management plan.

The shark is currently listed "Near Threatened" on the IUCN list although it may move to the vulnerable category before too long.

The lemon shark is thought to be of little danger to humans and there have only ever been a handful of unprovoked attacks. None of these attacks have been fatal despite the shark's close proximity to humans who are swimming or enjoying other water-based activities in enclosed bays and rivers.

With its blunt snout, the lemon shark looks remarkably like the bull shark, however, its second dorsal fin is much smaller than the first. The lemon shark's dorsal fins are similar to that of the sand tiger shark, but the latter shark is easily identifiable by its open mouth and needle-like teeth.

Chapter 19

Mako Shark

THE MAKO SHARK, ALONG WITH the blacktip reef shark, tiger shark, dogfish shark and thresher shark is caught off the Atlantic coast and can be found in seafood markets. The mako is one of the most popular sharks in the markets across the US and is a versatile dish that is typically prepared in steak form.

The shortfin mako is a stream-lined spindle-shaped shark that has a long pointed snout, large eyes and virtually closed jaws. It is coloured dark blue on its back while its underside is whitish. The mako is a pelagic – open water – shark that lives in deep water and has an average body length of around six to eight feet. Females typically have a longer life span than males and generally grow longer and heavier.

Considered one of the fastest sharks, it has a body which is designed for swimming and it is able to jump incredibly high – up to 20 feet – out of the water. The mako can reach speeds of up to 22mph although some reports state their speed at 31mph. Both types of mako species are renowned for their dynamic body shape and a powerful muscle mass which makes them faster and more agile than other shark species. A particularly dark-coloured shortfin mako is found only in the Azores and is similar in body to the longfin mako. The name mako usually means "large blue shark" although it can also mean "man eater". It is also known as a mackerel shark, paloma, bonito or springlio shark.

On the northeast Atlantic, the shortfin mako is abundant and favours the northern parts of its range during the hot summer months. The shark is also found off the coasts of Ireland, Cornwall including the Scilly Isles,

MAKO SHARK

mako is also familiar in the Mediterranean in offshore waters along the coast of Sicily, and Malta. It is less common in the Adriatic Sea but does have ranges in the Aegean Sea around Crete, Cyprus and Turkey.

The longfin mako also has a wide range and is found in the temperate and tropical seas and oceans of the world. This highly active shark is often found at a depth of around 150 metres and is sometimes seen nearer inshore, particularly around islands and islets which lie adjacent to deep water drop-offs near coastal reefs with abundant food sources. Shortfin mako sharks will follow warm water, but they keep within the confines of a specific geographical area. Very little is known about the social habits and mating rituals of these sharks, but it is widely documented that they are solitary fish.

The typical diet for both shortfin and longfin makos consists of mackerel, squid, tuna, swordfish and other smaller sharks. They have also been known to prey on sea turtles and rays. Adult makos have also been known to attack dolphins and they are prevalent around netted fish and harpooned fish – such as swordfish – that are being

Devon, Wales and occasionally as far as the Isle of Wight. Even more rare, the mako can sporadically be found in the North Sea and can reach as far as Norway, although this is extremely rare during the winter months. The shortfin mako is particularly prevalent in the Bay of Biscay, Spain and Portugal where the range spreads southwards to the tropics and oceanic islands. The

hunted. Swordfish are an adversary for the mako and care must be taken when hunting this particular prey.

At around three metres in length females become sexually mature. The mako is an ovoviviparous shark and females produce eggs which are nurtured in the uterus by a yolk sac. Shortfin mako embryos will consume each other in the mother's body in order to gain nutrients. This is called intrauterine cannibalism.

Gestation is between 15 and 18 months. Litters usually have between four and 18 surviving pups that are roughly 70cm at birth. Born in the late winter and early spring these juveniles are ready to begin their predatory life from the moment they're born without the support of their mother.

As well as being fished commercially, due to their sheer speed and agility, makos are a popular game fish, although once landed, they are a fairly dangerous catch for the fishermen due to their size and muscle power. In Ireland, the mako is much sought after as a gaming fish, but is rarely caught on a regular basis due to its short time in the waters off the island's coastline. Makos are generally found in these waters from late summer. The mako leaps out of the water when it is hooked. Fishermen use at least 30lb rods and reels for game fishing and a wire trace is an essential accessory while mackerel is the usual bait.

Chapter 20

Megamouth Shark

SOME EXPERTS ARGUE THAT THE megamouth shark shares a common ancestor with the basking shark, while others disagree and claim this great shark is more closely related to the mako, great white and porbeagle sharks. However, the megamouth shark does share the filter feeding system with the basking shark.

The megamouth has a stout, tapered body, a bulbous head and a particularly short snout. Its mouth is extremely broad and the corners of the mouth extend behind the eyes. The shark also has relatively low dorsal fins and the second is less than half the size of the first. In the adult megamouth, the pectoral fins are actually smaller than the length of the head while the top of the tail fin is a pronounced lobe. Megamouths are coloured black to brown while the pelvic fins are spectac-

ularly white. Both male and female megamouths have a curious white band across the snout which is particularly prominent when the upper jaw is protruded. The mouth has around 50 rows of small teeth in each jaw, but only three rows are actually functional. The average size of both males and females is around 17 feet.

The megamouth is found in the Atlantic, Pacific and Indian Oceans and like the basking and whale sharks – also filter feeders – the range is greatly distributed. It has been more noticeably spotted off the coasts of Hawaii, California, the Philippines, Senegal, Indonesia, Japan, western Australia and in both the temperate and tropical waters of the Pacific Ocean.

The megamouth is generally considered to be less active and a poorer swimmer than its counter-parts and it

has a flabby body which probably reflects this. The megamouth is a pelagic – open water – shark, however sightings and reports of this fairly large creature are few and far between.

There have only been 38 captured with accompanying documentation of megamouths and out of these, only two, give any real insight into the behaviour and social habits of this extraordinary shark. The sixth megamouth to be documented was in 1990 in California when a male was tagged and tracked for two days. It was discovered that the megamouth rests at the bottom of the ocean during the day and surfaces at night – known as vertical migration – to feed. This is probably the megamouth's response to following the shrimp (krill) that vertically migrate and on which

this great shark feeds. The megamouth is not a particularly buoyant shark and has an increased liver function to compensate for this. The only other sighting that has proved invaluable so far is the 13th where a megamouth was spotted in Indonesia in 1998 being attacked by sperm whales where it appeared confused at the surface of the water.

As the megamouth has not been greatly studied, complete details of its feeding patterns are not known, but it is thought that by swimming slowly – like the basking shark – the shark is able to catch huge volumes of shrimp and other prey as it moves through the water. Prey is caught by the megamouth's ability to "suck" in its food. Once the prey is safely inside the shark's mouth, the megamouth retracts its upper jaw and shuts its mouth.

Experts are also undecided about the origins for filter feeding in the megamouth. While some think that this method is closely related to that employed by basking sharks, others argue that filter feeding in both sharks evolved individually.

is the cookie cutter shark. This "parasite" latches onto the megamouth with its suction-like mouth and neatly rotates itself around the victim in order to take a perfectly symmetrical bite-sized chunk of flesh from the larger shark. Like other sharks – including the Greenland shark – the megamouth is also prone to other parasites such as worms and copepods (common in Greenland sharks).

The megamouth was first spotted in 1976 and is not commercially fished due to its rarity. As so little is known about the shark, it is not even considered to have enough data to give it a listing on the IUCN list. Currently it is defined as "Data Deficient". This shark is considered the most rare of all the shark species. Study of this shark is extremely important, however, as already mentioned only 38 specimens have ever been captured.

The first megamouth to be captured was on 15 November 1976 by a US Army vessel. As the megamouth had never been seen before, its discovery shocked the scientific world and the capture and subsequent examination of the shark became one of the most exciting events of the 20th century for marine biology.

The male megamouth shark is thought to bite down on the female during mating due to injuries and scars sustained and scientists have established that mating probably occurs off the coast of southern California during the autumn. Some research has led experts to believe that megamouths are probably ovoviviparous meaning that eggs are developed and hatched in the mother's uterus.

Apart from one incident where sperm whales were observed attacking a megamouth, another threat to this large shark

Chapter 21

Nurse Shark

THE NURSE SHARK, GINGLYOST-oma cirratum, is a shark in the nurse sharks family, the only member of its genus Ginglymostoma. It should not be confused with the grey nurse shark which is a much more aggressive creature. The nurse shark family name, Ginglymostomatidae, derives from the Greek words meaning hinge and mouth.

The origins of its name have been lost in the mists of time. One theory is that they were so named because they make a sucking sound that is a little like the sound of a nursing baby but the most popular definition is that it relates to the word Nusse, which the cat sharks of the family Scyliorhinidae – to which the nurse shark was once thought to belong – were called. Indeed, in some areas of the Caribbean, the nurse shark is still called the cat shark.

The nurse shark was originally thought to be related to the cat shark because of the long barbels (thin, fleshy, whisker-like organs that sense touch and taste) on its lower jaw in front of its nostrils which resemble those of a catfish. The first of its two spineless, rounded dorsal fins is larger than the second. It has one anal fin and a caudal fin that accounts for more than a quarter of the shark's length. Behind each eye there is a spiracle, an organ that takes in water used for breathing when the shark rests at the bottom, and the fourth and fifth gills are set very close together.

The skin ranges from light yellow to dark grey/brown on top and some nurse sharks, especially the young, have spots. Unlike most sharks, the nurse shark is smooth to the touch but it can grow to a respectable size of around four metres long. Sexual maturity is reached once

the sharks attain a length of just over two metres and nurse sharks are an ovoviviparous species. Males swim towards the females who are resting either on or just above the sea bed, before biting her and attempting to roll her over on to her side. Numerous males will attempt to mate with a female during the mating season but the females will soon have had enough and will be burying their pectoral fins in the ground in a show of defiance. The embryos develop inside

NURSE SHARK

the mother, who has a biennial reproductive cycle. The young are then born with 30-40 other pups by November or December and have a good chance of reaching the respectable age of 15-20.

The nurse shark is a large, sluggish, bottom-dwelling shark that is prevalent in the tropical and sub-tropical waters on the continental and insular shelves of the Atlantic and eastern Pacific Oceans. Reports of sightings have been made from Senegal, Brazil, Mexico and Peru while the species is very common in the shallow waters of Florida, the Florida Keys and throughout the West Indies. Unlike other shark species, nurse sharks do not migrate when the temperature cools they just suffer from decreased levels of activity.

The nurse shark is a nocturnal creature that rests with up to 40 others during the day in caves or rock crevices as well as on the sea bed. By night, they scour the sea looking for food in the form of stingrays, spiny lobsters, crabs, shrimps, sea urchins, octopi and squid while they can also extract snails from the shells using the suction produced by their small mouth. They also use the cover of darkness to catch small fish that usually rest at night.

Nurse sharks utilise independent dentition whereby there is no overlap between the teeth and they have thousands of replaceable teeth arranged in rows that rotate into position when a new one is needed (when older ones are broken or lost). These teeth, which are serrated and fan shaped, are capable of crushing shellfish. Due to their size and the localities they inhabit, they do not have any specific predators to be aware of, just large sharks basically. Tiger sharks and lemon sharks have been found with nurse sharks in their stomachs and it is not uncommon for them to be attacked by hammerhead sharks.

Nurse sharks are unlikely to attack humans and will normally swim away. Although some attacks have been reported, there have been no fatalities. Indeed, the nurse shark is probably the species that thrives most in captivity and tourists flock to where these fish can be found in shallow waters so they can handle and feed them.

The nurse shark is not commercially fished for either its meat or fins, although it has been considered a pest and its numbers have decreased over recent years, it is not yet classed as an endangered species.

Chapter 22

Porbeagle Shark

THE PORBEAGLE, LAMNA NASUS, takes its name from the Cornish dialect with porgh-bugel reportedly derived from porpoise (for its shape) and beagle (for its hunting abilities). First described as far back as 1788, the porbeagle belongs to the Lamniform order of sharks also known as mackerel sharks which also includes great whites, threshers and the megamouth.

While common in the southern hemisphere, the porbeagle is only found in the Atlantic Ocean in the northern hemisphere. Their habitat ranges from New Jersey to Canada and Greenland on the western side of the ocean and from the Mediterranean Sea right up through Iceland and Norway to Russia in the east. Its close relative, the salmon shark, only inhabits the northern Pacific Ocean.

The porbeagle is primarily a pelagic (open water) shark, but it has been spotted in both inshore and offshore waters (up to a depth of around 700 metres) and one was even caught in an Argentinian estuary but it has not been recorded as entering any fresh water source. Preferring cold water 1°C-18°C, it is predominant between 30°S and 60°S and has been known to inhabit waters as warm as 23°C. It is also believed to migrate to waters where it finds the temperature more suitable as the seasons change.

The most distinguishing characteristic of the porbeagle is a white patch on the trailing edge of the dorsal fin. This distinguishes it from both the salmon shark and the great white shark. It has two keels on its crescent-shaped caudal fin, in common with the salmon shark. The porbeagle is a stout and heavy shark, dark blue-grey on top and white underneath, with a conical snout. There is also a difference in colour between the northern and southern hemisphere porbeagles with the northern sharks sporting a white ventral surface on the head while their southern counterparts are dark in that area.

The porbeagle can grow to nearly four metres, weigh up to 250kg and live for around 30 years. In the northern hemisphere, porbeagle males mature at just over one and a half metres or eight years of age. There is a difference in maturation in the females of both hemispheres, with northern females at nearly two and a half metres or 13 years of age while their southern hemisphere cousins only have to reach nearly two metres before they are sexually active.

During mating, the male bites the female to keep her still and scientists find this a useful observation tool for being able to tell whether a female has recently mated. The porbeagle is ovoviviparous and fertilised eggs are carried by the mother for eight or nine months with no direct way of nourishing her youngsters. The embryos, however, engage in oophagy meaning they feed on unfertilised eggs produced by the ovary while still inside the mother's uterus which is divided into two branches.

The pups eventually arrive in the world in a litter of between one and six in spring or summer in the northern hemisphere and winter in the southern. They must then learn to survive on their own in their dangerous habitat. Although quite a large creature themselves, the porbeagles must be wary of attack from large sharks and mammals such as orcas (killer whales). The porbeagles' diet is predominantly bony fish – such as mackerel, herring, lancetfish and sauries – along with squid and groundfish like

sand lances, flounders, hakes and cod. The porbeagle is one of those few sharks – like the spinner shark – that can leap vertically out of the water.

Like all the other mackerel sharks, the porbeagles have a special blood circulatory system that is designed to help them regulate their own body temperature. They have counter-current heat exchangers which enable them to retain the heat their body's metabolic processes have generated. This is extremely useful in colder climates and the porbeagle can raise its body temperature to 10ºC above the external water.

Although attacks on people by porbeagles are not totally unknown, there have been no reported fatalities.

Although in abundance until recently, the porbeagle population has been in severe decline. Many sharks have been caught up as by-catch of commercial fishing but they are also hunted for their meat, fins and oils. It is also deemed a challenge by big game fishermen in the US, Canada – where they employ a catch and release policy, Ireland and the United Kingdom.

The porbeagle is listed as "Near Threatened" on the IUCN List of Threatened Species wherever it is located. That has been upped to "Vulnerable" in the north Atlantic, while Canada lists them as an endangered species. Over-fishing has recently decimated numbers in British waters.

Chapter 23

Spinner Shark

THE SPINNER SHARK, CARCHARH-inus brevipinna, is a requiem shark of the family Carcharhinidae – that includes the tiger shark, blue shark, bull shark and milk shark among others – that is often confused with the blacktip shark. The name comes from the Greek words karcharos meaning sharpen and rhinos meaning nose and it's easy to see why as the spinner shark is slim with a narrow, pointed snout. It also has small round eyes, long gill slits, small, narrow-cusped teeth and the first dorsal fin is small. There is no inter-dorsal ridge and the labial furrows are longer than in any other grey shark.

Colouration of the spinner shark is grey or bronze above and white underneath with a thin white band along their its flanks. The second dorsal, anal, undersides of pectorals and lower caudal fin lobe are black or dark grey-tipped in adults, but unmarked in juveniles. These markings can determine whether it is actually a spinner shark or a blacktip shark but, be aware, the markings can fade once the fish has died.

The teeth of the two species also differ with the Blacktip blacktip having broad teeth that recurve forward. The spinner shark has narrow, triangular teeth in the upper jaw and more slender teeth in the lower jaw which has a distinct notch. The tips of the teeth are not recurved forward, but slightly oblique.

The spinner shark can be found in the western Atlantic Ocean – around North Carolina, the Gulf of Mexico, the Bahamas, Cuba, Brazil and Argentina. It also ranges in the eastern Atlantic – from Spain – the Mediterranean Sea, and the Red Sea and before travelling around the Indo-Pacific areas of South Africa, Indonesia, Japan and Australia. Primarily a resident of sub-tropical waters, the spinner shark is found mainly between latitudes of 40°N and 40°S, covering both inshore and off-shore waters up to a depth of 100 metres. They are not found in the island regions of the Pacific.

Getting its name from its method of hunting, the spinner shark opens its mouth before spinning up through a school of fish, snapping its mouth in all directions. It can leap vertically out of the water. Again, it can be confused with the blacktip shark who is also capable of this feat. The main diet of the spinner shark is pelagic fish such as sardines, herrings, anchovies, ten-pounders, grunts, bluefish and tuna but it is also partial to stingrays, cuttlefish, octopi and squid. It has been known to devour fish that have been thrown overboard from fishing boats.

Spinner sharks grow on average to a length of two metres, weighing about 55kg, but some specimens have been known to reach just under three metres and 90kg. The largest specimens are to be found in the Indian Ocean and the Indo-Pacific, with smaller individuals observed in the northwestern Atlantic.

Females and males reach sexual maturity at around the same time when they are a little over one and a half metres long. Being viviparous, the embryos are fed via a yolk sac and placenta during their 12-15 month gestation period. The young fish are then born in the summer with the litter ranging from three to 15 pups and each pup can be up to 75cm long.

Once the juveniles are born, they head straight for the shallow waters of an estuary or inlet where there is ample supply of food and more likelihood of them evading an attack from predators. Due to their smaller size, they are often preyed upon by larger sharks but if they survive the initial dangers spinner sharks can live for around 20 years.

Perhaps because of their size, spinner sharks form schools to enjoy safety in numbers and are particularly migratory off Florida, Louisiana and in the Gulf of Mexico. Here the sharks move inshore for the spring and summer where they feed and reproduce.

Although there have been no documented fatalities following an attack on humans, the International Shark Attack File does have reports on 13 unpro-

voked attacks by spinner sharks. With its small teeth, it is used to feeding on small fish so it is possible that these divers or swimmers were wearing something – a watch or jewellery – that caught the light's reflection and gave the shark the impression that light was glinting off a fish's scales.

Spinner sharks are commonly caught on long lines by commercial fisheries but also end up as a by-catch.

Like most sharks, the fins end up in shark- fin soup and their skin is sold as leather but the flesh of the spinner shark is dried and salted before it is deemed appetising enough for human consumption. They are also a prized catch in big game fishing with anglers desperate to hook one because the shark will make two or three hard, long runs before the angler can get their head turned toward the boat.

Chapter 24

Thresher Shark

NAMED FOR THEIR DISTINCTIVE long tail or caudal fin that is sometimes as long as their body length, the thresher shark belongs to the Lamniform order of sharks also known as mackerel sharks which includes great whites and the megamouth. Characteristics of the order include two dorsal fins, an anal fin, five gill slits, eyes without nictitating membrane and mouth extending behind the eyes. They also possess a special circulatory system that can raise their body temperature in relation to the water surrounding them, enabling them to survive in cooler climates.

The genus and family name derive from the Greek word alopex, meaning fox. Indeed the long-tailed thresher shark, Alopias vulpinus, is named the fox shark by some authorities. They are also commonly known as foxtail, sickletail, swingletail and swiveltail sharks. There

are three species of thresher shark: the common thresher, the bigeye thresher – named for the huge eye that is set high in its head – and the pelagic thresher.

The common thresher shark is found in tropical and cold-temperate waters around the world. Its habitat ranges from the Atlantic Ocean (from Newfoundland to Cuba, Brazil to Argentina and Europe to the Ivory Coast), the Mediterranean Sea, the Indian Ocean (Pakistan, India and Sri Lanka) and the Pacific Ocean (from Australasia to British Columbia and Chile). Rarely sighted in shallow waters, the adult common thresher shark prefers swimming on the continental shelves of North America and Asia in 500 metres of water while the bigeye and pelagic thresher sharks are more prevalent in central and western Pacific areas and are usually not found below a

depth of 150 metres.

The thresher shark can easily be recognised by its caudal fin that sports an extremely long upper lobe. This fin can be used as a weapon and thresher sharks can stun their intended victim with a swipe of their tail. Thresher sharks are a slender fish with a small first dorsal fin ahead of the pelvic fins. Their pectoral fins are curved and taper to a point (i.e. sickle-shaped, hence the name sickletail shark). The bigeye thresher also boasts a V-shaped forehead ridge and a longer snout while the pelagic thresher's pectoral fins are almost straight. Threshers have a medium sized eye with the exception

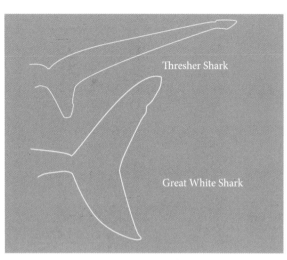

of the bigeye variety.

Threshers are commonly brown or grey but can be nearly totally black with a white belly and the three species can normally be distinguished by the main colour of the dorsal surface of the body. Common threshers are dark green, bigeye threshers are brown and pelagic threshers are generally blue although lighting conditions and water clarity can affect how any one shark appears.

Size of thresher sharks varies by species but the pelagic thresher is the smallest at three metres long. The big-

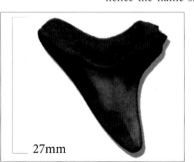

27mm

eye thresher can reach a length of five metres while the largest is the common thresher which has been recorded at nearly eight metres and can weigh around 350kg.

Like many other species of shark, thresher sharks are slow in reaching maturity with males being seven to 13 years old and females eight to 14 years of age before they begin to reproduce annually. Thresher sharks are another ovoviviparous species – the embryo develops without a placenta – and, once the young fish have obtained all the nourishment they can from their yolk sacs, they begin feasting on their mother's unfertilised eggs. They are born into a litter of between two and four pups and are around four to five feet long, giving them an extremely good chance of survival with some individuals living as long as 20 years.

They feed mainly on bony fish such as bluefish, butterfish, small tuna, herring and mackerel but have also been known to devour squid, crustaceans and sea birds. Thresher sharks often hunt together, either in pairs or groups, and will circle the school of fish before they swing their tails to stun their prey. This method of attack works just as well on unwary birds floating on the sea but thresher sharks have also been known to jump out of the water – as a dolphin would – in an activity known as breaching.

Adult thresher sharks do not have any known predators, but they can fall prey to larger sharks and other mammals. Juveniles have a particularly hard time making it through to adulthood.

The common and pelagic threshers are hunted as a source of food – the flesh of the bigeye thresher is deemed too mushy to be appetising – oil, leather and sport but are more often by-catch. There is currently not enough information available to the IUCN to determine how vulnerable this species is so they have classified it as "Data Deficient" but it is hoped that research over the next few years will provide a true picture of the thresher shark's plight.

Chapter 25

Tiger Shark

COMMONLY KNOWN BY OTHER names such as the leopard shark, man eater shark or spotted shark, the tiger shark is the second most dangerous behind the great white shark in terms of number of reported attacks on humans. Tiger sharks have been reported to prey on people who have been surfing or snorkelling less than 100 yards from the shore…there was even one report of an eight-year-old boy being attacked while standing in the surf in Florida in 1934.

Indeed, such was the danger from tiger sharks around Hawaii that more than 4,500 were hunted and killed between 1959 and 1976 – despite being considered to be sacred "aumakua" or ancestor spirits by the native Hawaiians – because it was proving to be detrimental to the tourist industry.

Tiger sharks live mainly in the world's tropical and sub-tropical waters, although they have been known to favour more temperate climates and some individuals have even followed the Gulf Stream to Iceland and the United Kingdom. They are more likely to be found in the warmer waters around the Equator during winter months and dive to a maximum depth of 350 metres.

It was first described in 1822 and was later classified as the only member of the genus Galeocerdo. Galeocerdo is derived from the Greek galeos which means shark and the Latin cerdus which means the hard hairs of pigs.

Nicknamed "the wastebasket of the sea" due to the fact that car number plates and bits of tyres have been found in specimens' stomachs, the tiger shark prefers river estuaries and harbours where prey is more plentiful. Their usual diet, however, includes sea birds, dolphins, seals, squid, sea turtles, rays, other sharks, bony fish and crustaceans. They are also well known for eating carrion and have been found with human body parts inside them.

The tiger shark has evolved to sport serrated teeth which enables it to tear chunks from its prey. These teeth, and the jaws they are set in, are very strong which enables the shark to bite through a turtle shell or bone. They are very aggressive and have been reported circling their prey, nudging it with their snouts to see what reaction they will get.

Tiger sharks are one of the largest shark species, belonging to the Carcharhinidae family that includes some of the best-known and most common types of sharks such as the blue

TIGER SHARK

shark, bull shark, and milk shark. They have the usual carcharhiniform characteristics with round eyes and their pectoral fins are completely behind the five gill slits. They are usually blue-green, dark grey or black on top and yellowish white underneath. The young feature spots and stripes that fade as they get older.

Although their average size is up to four metres with a weight of around 600kg, this species has the ability to grow to over seven metres long and weigh more than 1,500kg. Featuring a wedge-shaped head that aids the shark when making quick changes of direction, the tiger shark has long fins that provide lift through the water and a long upper tail that can propel it at speeds of around 20mph.

Males reach sexual maturity at seven to nine feet whereas females need to be around eight to ten feet and mating usually occurs during March and May in the northern hemisphere and towards the end of the year in the southern hemisphere. The male bites the female to hold her steady and inserts one of his claspers – which developed from its pelvic fin – into the female's genital opening. The mother gives birth to between 10 and 80 live pups – the tiger shark is the only one of its family to be ovoviviparous – sized at 51-76cm long after a 14-16 month gestation period. The juveniles are immediately sent out into the ocean to fend for themselves. Some scientists believe that the mother produces uterine milk while the young are developing and that accounts for their size at birth. Again, it is not definitely known how long tiger sharks live for, but a conservative estimate is 20 years.

With its reputation as a man eater, the tiger shark is routinely hunted as a big game fish. It is not commercially fished, but is killed for its liver – high in Vitamin A – fins and skin. A tiger shark's skin is sturdy, makes quality leather and is considered exotic for its striped tiger-like appearance, making it ideal for fashion accessories such as handbags. Although catch rates for this species reduced in the latter half of the 20th century – possibly indicating that they had been over-fished – the IUCN has the tiger shark listed as "Not Threatened". However many there are in the world's oceans, they must always be treated with respect for the killing machine they undoubtedly are.

TIGER SHARK

Chapter 26

Whale Shark

THE FIRST SPECIMEN OF A WHALE shark was harpooned in South Africa's Table Bay, being described and named in 1828. Classified in the Orectolobiformes order – with family members such as nurse sharks and wobbegongs – it is perhaps surprising that it took until the early 19th century for this to occur as whale sharks are very widespread and enjoy all tropical and warm temperate seas where the water temperature ranges from 21-30°C. In fact, one of the few places that this species is not found is the Mediterranean. They inhabit the warm waters of the Atlantic Ocean (from New York down to the Caribbean and Brazil), the Indian Ocean, the Arabian Gulf and around California, Chile, Hawaii, Australia and Japan.

A pelagic – open water – dweller, the whale shark is regularly seen off the western coast of Australia between the full

moons in March and April. This concentration of the species occurs in that location each year to feed on the vast amounts of zooplankton that are associated with coral spawning. It is believed that these sharks are migratory although further research must be undertaken before this can be confirmed.

The most distinctive feature of a whale shark is its enormous V-shaped mouth (with each jaw containing around 300 tiny teeth), located near the tip of the snout, which is vital for feeding. The whale shark's diet consists mainly of plankton, supplemented by small crustaceans, schools of smaller fish and sometimes tuna or squid. The shark opens its mouth and moves its head from side to side once it has found its plankton source, sucking water in and pushing it out through its gills – unlike the basking shark which uses its

forward momentum to force water into its mouth – where the tiny organisms are filtered and the water expelled.

It has a broad head and a streamlined body, with the first dorsal fin noticeably larger than the second, and grows to a size of around 20 metres.

The colouration of a whale shark is distinctive as well, with the upper body (that is brown, blue or grey) being covered by a pattern of vertical and horizontal pale stripes making a chequered effect. This camouflage – also believed

to help shield the shark from ultraviolet radiation while it is swimming near the surface – is further aided by the creamy white spots that are housed within these squares. As is typical of surface fish, the whale shark's underside is white which helps to avoid detection from predators below.

As the world's largest living fish, their predators are few and far between – unless the shark is aged or infirm – and it is estimated that they can live to be 60 years old but whale sharks have been found in the stomachs of blue sharks and blue marlins. They reach sexual maturity at about nine metres in length and it was finally discovered in 1995 that they are ovoviviparous when an 11 metre female was killed near Taiwan. She was bearing 300 young, between 42 and 63cm, and would have been heading for the waters of the Kuroshio Current – the world's second largest ocean current after the Gulf Stream – which is an important birthing area that runs from the east coast of Taiwan northwards to Japan.

The World Conservation Union does not have enough information on whale sharks to be able to definitely categorise the danger that the species faces and have given them "Indeterminate" status on their Red List of Threatened Animals. The whale shark has, however, been classified as "Vulnerable" on the

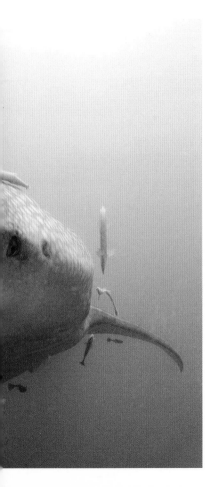

IUCN's lists and its population suffers greatly from its slow growth, long life and the fact that individuals cannot reproduce for such a long time after birth. They are not endangered in the Gulf of California but legislation has been introduced banning them from being fished in the Maldives and the Philippines.

While whale sharks can suffer from over-fishing – their meat is particularly sought after in Taiwan and their liver oil is often used to waterproof boats – they have recently been exploited in areas where they can be almost guaranteed to be found. Although they are more often than not solitary creatures, they have been found in groups numbering as much as 100. Tourism can mean big money but conservation plans have been implemented in places like Australia's Ningaloo Reef to limit the number of tour operators. Divers have not reported any serious incidents while on these excursions with the whale shark merely diving deeper to avoid contact with humans. Although whale sharks have been known to butt small boats when provoked, tourists are requested not to harass these gentle giants of the deep but simply enjoy their graceful beauty.

ALSO AVAILABLE IN THIS SERIES

The pictures in this book were provided courtesy of the following:

GETTY IMAGES
101 Bayham Street, London NW1 0AG

SHUTTERSTOCK IMAGES
www.shutterstock.com

Design and artwork by David Wildish

Creative Director Kevin Gardner

Published by Green Umbrella Publishing

Publishers Jules Gammond and Vanessa Gardner

Written by Louise Malo